THE THRU-HIKER'S PLANNING GUIDE

Dan "Wingfoot" Bruce

Workbook Edition

CENTER FOR APPALACHIAN TRAIL STUDIES

"WHERE THRU-HIKERS COME FIRST"

The Thru-hiker's Planning Guide

© Copyright 1994 Dan Bruce
All rights reserved

No part of this work may be reproduced or transmitted in any form by any means, electronic or mechanical, including photocopying and recording or any information storage-and-retrieval system, for any purpose other than the individual purchaser's private use, without written permission from the author, who is solely responsible for the content of *The Thru-hiker's Planning Guide*. Capitalized brand and product names used in the text of this work are registered trademarks unless noted otherwise.

Center for Appalachian Trail Studies
P. O. Box 525
Hot Springs, North Carolina 28743

Library of Congress Catalog Card Number: 94-70565
ISBN 0-9636342-3-2

Printed in the United States of America

Workbook Edition

The Center for Appalachian Trail Studies is an informal organization founded in 1993 to provide user-friendly interpretive publications about the Appalachian Trail to the hiking public, with special emphasis on long-distance hiking and serving the specific needs of long-distance hikers. Proceeds from the sale of this book are used to support the programs of the Center. For information about our other publications, seminars, and special events, and for general information about the Appalachian Trail, call (704) 622-7601, Monday through Friday, between 10:30 a.m. and 6:30 p.m., Eastern Time.

THE THRU-HIKER'S PLANNING GUIDE

Contents

Introduction 1

The Appalachian Trail 3

Deciding to Thru-hike 5

How to Begin Planning 7

1 Guidebooks and Maps 10

2 Equipment 15

3 Footwear 26

4 Clothing 29

5 Food and Supplies 33

6 Health and Hygiene 39

7 Scheduling and Maildrops 44

8 Budgeting and Finances 50

9 Miscellaneous Topics 53

10 Last-Minute Preparations 58

Sample Planning Notebook 59

Post Office Information 83

Table of Town Services 85

Climate and Weather Chart 87

Trail Food Calorie Chart 88

Thru-hiker's Product Guide 89

Workbook Section 95

Introduction

The Appalachian Trail, by its very length, excites the sense of adventure in every hiker. The possibility of hiking it from one end to the other has obviously fired your imagination even further. That being the case, welcome to the world of A.T. thru-hiking. Be assured, you are entering a community of men and women with a long and proud hiking tradition.

The A.T. was completed from Georgia to Maine in 1937. Once linked, hiking the whole thing from end to end became an immediate challenge. In those early years, veteran and novice hikers alike dreamed of being the first to do the Trail in one continuous journey, and a few made admirable attempts, but no one was able to go the distance. For more than a decade thereafter, such a trip was considered by most to be an impossible feat, too rugged and demanding for any individual. Then, in 1948, Earl Shaffer of Pennsylvania accomplished the impossible. He hiked the entire Appalachian Trail in a remarkably swift 124 days. His thru-hike was a marvelous personal achievement—in hiking terms the equivalent of Lindbergh's solo flight across the Atlantic. And like the Lindbergh flight, Earl's hike blazed the way for other hardy souls to follow. Starting with a few hikers a year in the 1950s and 1960s, the parade of thru-hikers swelled to hundreds a year in the 1970s, a trend that has continued to the present. Since 1948, more than 20,000 people have set out to hike the entire A.T. in one journey, with about one in ten of them making it all the way. Today, the Appalachian Trail Conference lists more than 2,800 people as "2000-Milers," and I am pleased to be among their number.

No one is born knowing the ins and outs of backpacking, of course, and I was no exception. My lack of experience was apparent in 1980 on my first overnight A.T. backpacking trip, which was, in hindsight, the proverbial comedy of errors. Nevertheless, I enjoyed that trip immensely and, sometime during that initial hike, the idea of one day exploring the Trail from end to end grabbed hold of my imagination. Over the next few years, the dream grew into an obsession, so in early 1984, unable to resist the lure of the Trail any longer, I started making preparations to do a thru-hike the following summer. Ten months later, when my plans were complete—and admittedly with far more bravado than confidence—I shouldered my pack on April 23, 1985, and departed from Georgia's Springer Mountain to begin my adventure. The odyssey that unfolded as I headed up the Trail was the most exciting and challenging experience of my life, and I will never forget the feeling of satisfaction when, five months later, I climbed Katahdin in Maine to complete my trek. Since that first hike, I have hiked the entire A.T. six more times, observing and interacting with more than 10,000 fellow thru-hikers along the way. Using the knowledge and perspective gained on my hikes, I have had the additional pleasure of helping several thousand people plan their end-to-end hikes.

The Thru-hiker's Planning Guide is, in large part, a compilation of the material shared with the many soon-to-be thru-hikers who have sought my help over the past few years. In its pages you will find virtually everything you need to know for planning a thru-hike. It shows you how to begin and organize your planning, and systematically discusses equipment, footwear, clothing, food and supplies, scheduling, maildrops, budgeting, and other topics pertinent to an end-to-end hike. In its planning chapters, it provides step-by-step instructions and offers helpful illustrations for reference as you plan. Though it does not contain any "secrets" that will guarantee the success of your venture (there aren't any), it does present you with a full range of planning options reflecting the things that have worked well for many recent thru-hikers and should work well for you. Keep in mind, however, that this guide intentionally does not tell you what choices to make as you do your planning. It gives you the basic planning information you need, respects your innate ability to discern what is best for you, and leaves all decision-making to you. Thus, by picking and choosing from the information and broad range of advice given, you will be able to plan a thru-hike tailored to your specific hiking style, preferences, and goals.

The Thru-hiker's Planning Guide

You are to be commended for choosing an A.T. thru-hike as the way to live life amid the splendors of nature for a season or so. I can assure you that the time you spend traversing the mountains and woods of eastern America will be everything you expect and more. This guide has been written in the hope that, by helping you make informed decisions and sensible choices before you begin your trek, you will be able to derive the utmost enjoyment from your journey. As you prepare for your adventure in the months to come, I am confident that you will discover what many others before you, including me, have found: Planning an Appalachian Trail thru-hike is a most rewarding experience, in its own special way almost as exhilarating as doing the hike itself.

—Dan "Wingfoot" Bruce

P.S.—I welcome comments, questions, and just plain "Trail talk" by telephone, if you can catch me when I am not either clicking away on my usually faithful computer or hiking on my currently favorite trail. You can reach me at (704) 622-7601, but please limit calls to the hours between 7:30 p.m. and 9:30 p.m., Eastern Time.

The Appalachian Trail

The Appalachian Trail is America's oldest continental-length recreational footpath, but not an updated version of an ancient Native American pathway as many prospective thru-hikers mistakenly believe. Instead, it has been built entirely in this century by thousands of dedicated volunteers—men and women who, over many years, have given of their time, sweat, muscles, and money to create a place where modern pilgrims can transit the mountains and commune with nature. Its route stretches approximately 2,150 miles from Springer Mountain in Georgia to Katahdin in Maine, generally following the ridge line of the eastern Appalachian chain through fourteen states, six national park units, eight national forests, and numerous other public and some private lands. Today, the A.T. is the premier component of the National Scenic Trails System established by Congress in 1968, and is operated under the authority of the National Park Service. The NPS has delegated management of the A.T. to the Appalachian Trail Conference, a nonprofit corporation, establishing what has become one of the most successful government/private-sector partnerships in America.

The Appalachian Trail Conference, known simply as "ATC" in hiking circles, has coordinated the design, building, and maintenance of the A.T. since the earliest days. From its headquarters in Harpers Ferry, West Virginia, the ATC coordinates activities of its member clubs and volunteer maintainers. Management of the footpath and its associated buffer zone is the organization's main mission. In addition, it serves as one of the Trail's information clearinghouses. As a thru-hiker with specific interests and needs, you will find that most ATC programs and priorities are focused elsewhere—on maintenance and club activities—and that most Conference publications are aimed at the general hiking audience. The Conference is governed by a Board of Managers elected by the members and has a full-time salaried staff that oversees daily operations. Members are kept informed about ATC activities through its magazine, the *Appalachian Trailway News*, and at a week-long meeting of the general membership which is held every two years. The ATC has thirty-two member clubs with 5,000 volunteer maintainers, the latter often referred to as "the heart and soul of the A.T. project." They are the ones who do most of the field work—building, relocating, and maintaining the footpath and its associated facilities, all without pay. The Trail, in many ways, is a gift from these people to you and me. The club volunteers are also involved in the management of surrounding lands, land-acquisition negotiations, compilation and updating of guidebooks, public relations with neighboring communities, and recruitment and training of maintainers.

The A.T. and its facilities are open year-round to the public for foot travel without restriction, and the footpath itself is open from Georgia to Maine at no cost to users. No official permission is required to thru-hike the Trail, either, but thru-hikers must self-register when entering Great Smoky Mountains and Shenandoah National Parks, and Maine's Baxter State Park reserves the right to deny thru-hikers permission to climb Katahdin if so doing is deemed dangerous due to weather conditions. On rare occasions, portions of the Trail are closed temporarily if there is danger to the public, as in the case of forest fires. Pack animals and wheeled vehicles are strictly prohibited. The official route of the A.T. is marked continuously from end to end by its trademark blazes, 2-inch-wide by 6-inch-high white rectangles painted on trees or rocks at regular intervals. Side trails to water sources, viewpoints, and other features are marked by blue blazes. A system of lean-to shelters, cost free to the public except in some high-use areas, spans the length of the Trail. These shelters are spaced a comfortable day's hiking distance apart on average—closer together in sections that have greater use. They come in a variety of designs and sizes, but all have raised sleeping platforms and many have cooking areas, picnic tables, and other conveniences. Several even have porches, and at least one has a swing. Outhouses for sanitation are usually located nearby. Springs or streams are commonly available as water sources at shelters and at many points between, with the distance between water sources averaging less than three or four miles.

The A.T. route goes through the center of more than a dozen towns and communities and comes close to many, so services needed by thru-hikers, such as telephones, lodging, grocery stores, and laundromats, are never very far away. Thru-hikers also frequently find that other hikers are never very far away, since about three million people use the A.T. each year. Most of these visitors are out doing day-hikes or weekend trips; some are doing longer trips during the vacation season. However, thru-hikers rarely feel overrun by other users. The Trail is a big place, allowing most people to maintain an illusion of isolation in the woods throughout their journey. In fact, thru-hikers often seem to each other to be the only people using the A.T., because most start from Georgia in late March or April and are concentrated together as they head northward. They come from almost every state and several foreign nations, especially the English-speaking countries, and reflect the spectrum of ages, occupations, and education and income levels that are seen in the general population. About twenty to thirty *per cent* are women.

The Appalachian Trail has long been this country's best known and most publicized hiking trail, with thru-hikers and thru-hikes accounting for most of the publicity. More than likely, you were encouraged to think about doing an end-to-end hike by a book, magazine or newspaper article, or television news feature that related some previous hiker's great adventure. Perhaps, in the future, your story will inspire others to follow in your footsteps.

Safety Considerations

All prospective thru-hikers should give thought to their safety on the Trail, inasmuch as the ills of society sometimes intrude on the normally idyllic A.T. environment. Incidents of harassment and more serious crimes have occurred in recent decades, usually in or near towns and along roads, and such occurrences are always a possibility. Concern for personal safety should be kept in perspective, however, since the A.T. is statistically one of the safest places in America, certainly far safer than the home towns of most thru-hikers. The Trail has no law enforcement of its own, so each hiker must assume responsibility for his or her own safety while on the footpath. Publications normally used by thru-hikers contain a section of safety precautions that should be read and observed by everyone using the Trail. These recommended safeguards depend on common sense, hiker awareness, and thinking defensively, and they are all that is needed for protection during a thru-hike. Firearms, large knives, Mace, guard dogs, and other defensive weapons are unnecessary, and they are illegal in some federal, state, and local jurisdictions through which the A.T. passes. In practice, few, if any, hikers encounter challenges to their persons from year to year. Personal safety is not a source of constant concern for most thru-hikers once they have hiked on the Trail for a few weeks and have seen how members of the thru-hiking community keep watch on one another. Equipment safety is not a major concern, either. Hikers generally observe a very strict code of honor when it comes to the equipment of others, and few instances of tampering or theft on the footpath itself have been reported over the years.

ATC Membership

Membership in the Appalachian Trail Conference is open to the general public, whether they hike or not. As a prospective thru-hiker, you should consider joining the ATC, at least for the year you will be doing your hike. As a member, you will receive a membership card, which will get you reduced rates at several facilities near the Trail during your hike; a cloth A.T. patch, which looks good on your pack or clothing during your hike; an A.T. bumper sticker, which may impress the neighbors who possibly think you are crazy for wanting to do a thru-hike; the right to attend and vote at the biennial general meeting of the organization; a subscription to the *Appalachian Trailway News*, the five-times a year magazine devoted to news and feature articles about the A.T., the Conference, and its members; and substantial discounts on Conference publications and A.T. paraphernalia (T-shirts, caps, patches, calendars, *etc.*), which can more than offset the cost of membership. For information, contact the Appalachian Trail Conference, P.O. Box 807, Harpers Ferry, West Virginia 25425, or call (304) 535-6331, Monday through Friday, between 9 a.m. and 5 p.m., Eastern Time.

Deciding to Thru-hike

The decision to attempt a thru-hike is one that requires you to commit a significant portion of your time and resources for many months. It is very important that you understand what will be required for doing an end-to-end hike before you make that commitment, and it is equally important that you feel confident about the likelihood of completing a thru-hike before you begin your planning. Consider the statistics. Several thousand people decide to hike the A.T. from end to end each year, and nine out of ten of them will have dropped out before the year is over. The primary reason so many of these adventurers fall short is that their decision to thru-hike was made impulsively, without considering the requirements for doing a 2,150-mile multi-month outdoor trip. All too often, even against their better judgement, they go ahead anyway. Then, at some point along the way, they find what they knew, or should have known, when they started—they do not have enough time, money, or some other ingredient necessary for finishing their journey. That is when they become dropouts instead of 2,000-Milers. Chances are you have already decided to attempt a thru-hike, or perhaps you are still trying to decide. Either way, you owe it to yourself to take a few minutes to review your decision, so that you will not knowingly start a journey you cannot finish. Using the discussion paragraphs that follow as criteria, take a realistic look at your situation and ask yourself if you think you have the basic requirements needed for doing an end-to-end hike.

Time: You will need at least five months to complete a thru-hike, assuming you have average hiking ability (average meaning you can maintain a pace of about 12-15 miles per day once you get into shape). If you can take six months, your hike will be even more enjoyable, because you will not have to push yourself to stay on schedule and will be able to take more rest days in towns. Four months is not enough time, unless you are an exceptionally strong hiker and want to do nothing but hike long miles day after day, foregoing much of the hiker social scene. Most thru-hikers take 160-195 days to complete their hikes. End-to-end hikes of this duration require steady hiking but allow ample time for smelling the roses as well.

Money: You will need a minimum of $2,200 (a dollar a mile) for a "normal" thru-hike, assuming you have already purchased all of your equipment and perhaps some of your food, and not taking into account your travel expenses to and from the Trailheads. For that amount, you can do a very fine hike. If you choose to do a Spartan trip with few overnight town stops and social amenities, you can budget a bit more modestly. If you elect to visit many towns, stay in motels rather than hostels, and eat often at restaurants, your expenses will be considerably greater. Most first-time thru-hikers end up spending more than the amount recommended above, usually because they choose to take more time off in towns and have bigger appetites than anticipated.

Health: You will need to be in good health to do a thru-hike, but health should not be confused with youth and athletic ability. People of all adult ages, and many folks with only modest athletic abilities, have hiked the entire Trail with no major problems. You will need to be in reasonably good physical condition before you begin your hike, but, here again, you do not need to be a trained athlete as long as you do not overdo it at the beginning. As for disease and disability, some otherwise healthy folks with such conditions as diabetes, epilepsy, and recent heart-bypass operations have made it all the way in good shape, so do not let such impediments automatically rule you out.

Experience: You should not let lack of previous hiking experience by itself be the deciding factor in your decision to do an end-to-end hike. A surprising number of novices do quite well on a thru-hike without ever having hiked a step on the A.T. or any other trail. Your instincts, adaptability, and prehike planning will be as important as experience. Nevertheless, common sense says that, the more hiking experience you have, the better your chances of having a successful thru-hike. If you can, take several practice hikes before you make your final decision to attempt a thru-hike. At least one practice hike should be for four days and nights. If you can handle a four-day trip, you can probably manage a thru-hike.

Desire: You should have an almost overwhelming desire to do a thru-hike, or likely you will not be able to repeatedly muster the tenacity and fortitude to keep hiking when the going gets rough, which it will on many occasions. A thru-hike is not an easy trip. Continuous hiking wears on you day after day and pushes you to your physical, mental, emotional, and even spiritual limits. Someone wisely said about the desire needed to do a thru-hike, "If thru-hiking the A. T. is not the most important goal in your life, at least right now, you may want to consider doing what is instead." If you do have overwhelming desire, you have the single most important element for doing an end-to-end hike.

Motives: Your principal motive for wanting to thru-hike should be to enjoy nature and live in simplicity and harmony with it. The A.T. was created for that express purpose—to allow men and women to get away from the complexities of modern life and seek fellowship with the wilderness. Secondary motives will undoubtedly include your quest for adventure and longing for camaraderie with others who share your love of the outdoors. If your reason for wanting to do a thru-hike is to gain personal attention and fame, to lead a crusade or fund-raising effort for your pet cause (no matter how worthy), or to engage in competitive activities or record-setting attempts designed to prove you are somehow better than your fellow thru-hikers, you would do better to find another venue.

If, after consideration, you are satisfied that you have or will have the ingredients necessary to attempt a thru-hike, you are ready to begin making your plans. If you do not feel you can handle a thru-hike, but still want to hike the whole A.T., you might consider doing it in sections over a period of time. Section-hiking is an alternative that has proven attractive to many people. You can use this guide for planning long section-hikes, too.

Suggested Reading and Videos

ATC Member Handbook (published by the ATC). The official introduction to Appalachian Trail Conference, containing a brief history of the Trail project and presenting the programs and structure of the organization.

Walking with Spring, by Earl V. Shaffer (published by the ATC). The narrative of the historic first A.T. thru-hike in 1948, told in simple prose and poetry by the man who did it.

Hiking the Appalachian Trail, edited by James R. Hare (Emmaus, Pa., Rodale Press, 1975, two vols.). The narratives of the first 46 people to hike the entire A.T. It is now out of print but available from many libraries and occasionally advertised for sale in the *Appalachian Trailway News*.

Mountain Adventure: Exploring the Appalachian Trail, by Ron Fisher (Washington, D.C., National Geographic Society, 1988). The story of the Appalachian Trail today, as interpreted by a writer and photographer Sam Abell of the National Geographic Society.

"The Appalachian Trail: Main Street, USA," by Jim Chase (*Backpacker*, September 1987).

"The Appalachian Trail: A Tunnel Through Time," by Noel Grove (*National Geographic*, February 1987).

Five Million Steps (Video), by Lynne Wheldon, 90 E. Union St., Canton, Pa. 17724. Fourteen 1986 thru-hikers are interviewed and shown hiking, one per Trail state, plus many scenes of places on the Trail.

Trail Magic (Video), by Carol Moore, P.O. Box 960, Laguna Beach, Calif. 92652. The A.T. Class of '90 as seen through the eyes of a 1989 thru-hiker. Interviews with dozens of hikers, plus scenes and sounds that capture the essence of the Trail experience.

How to Begin Planning

Planning a 2,150-mile hike can be a lot of fun, but, now that you have actually decided to attempt a thru-hike, you probably sense that planning it will also involve a fair amount of mental labor. You may feel somewhat dazed by the seeming complexity of all the details, and may even feel that planning your hike will be an enigmatic undertaking, one requiring numerous decisions (or even worse, guesses!) about things that are all too unclear. If it is any comfort, most past thru-hikers report feeling the same way. I was also overwhelmed as I began planning my first thru-hike. After several weeks of worrying about everything all at once and getting next to nothing accomplished, it dawned on me that I must do my planning in the same manner I would do my thru-hike—that is, in segments, taking one step at a time. Using my newly found insight, I set about to bring my planning under control, to develop a simple step-by-step approach to planning that would get me to the Trailhead fully prepared to do an end-to-end hike.

The first thing I did to simplify my planning was to break it down into its component parts. I started by asking myself the obvious questions: What equipment will I need? What will I eat? Where will I obtain food? How will I cook my food? Where will I sleep? How many miles should I hike each day? and so on. In the early stages, I still reverted to my initial state of near-panic from time to time, wondering if planning would ever make any sense. As I continued to ask common-sense questions, however, and began grouping together the questions that related to each other, everything gradually started to come into focus. The logical parts of planning a thru-hike began to emerge from the mass, and I began to get a clear view of which parts needed to be planned first. Next, I started planning the parts one by one. Soon I found that each part had questions of its own and discovered, as I continued to plan, that the remainder of my planning involved finding answers to these intrinsic questions. To do so, I usually had to go through a simple four-step procedure with each question, as follows: define the question, identify the range of possible answers (which usually meant gathering information), decide on the specific answer that best suited my needs, and then do whatever action my decision required once it was made.

For example, to answer the question about what items of equipment I would need to buy for my hike, I had to make a list of every piece of gear I thought would be necessary for a thru-hike, inventory the gear I already owned, and then compare the two. The comparison showed me that I needed, among other things, a new stove, but that raised another question: Which type of stove should I buy? Once this new question was defined, I began the process all over again, gathering information about backpacking stoves and my cooking requirements until I had enough data to make a wise decision. Then, I made my decision, bought a new stove, and moved on to finding answers to other questions until my planning was complete. The application of this simple procedure varied slightly from question to question, but the basic step-by-step process was repeated over and over again as I made my plans. By using the simple planning procedures just outlined, I was able to plan my first thru-hike (and all of my subsequent A.T. hikes) efficiently and with the assurance that I was making all necessary preparations for doing an end-to-end hike. This guide will help you do the same.

Using This Guide

Planning your thru-hike will be a process of dividing everything into its component parts, examining the planning options presented by each part, choosing which options best suit the way you want to do your hike, and then recording your choices on paper so that you can retrieve the information for later use when assembling everything needed to do your hike. This guide simplifies the planning process for you in several ways. Your overall planning has already been divided into its component parts, with each part indicated by one of this guide's ten numbered planning chapters. Each planning chapter, in turn, is organized to systematically lead you through the steps necessary to complete the planning that pertains to the chapter's topic. Following the planning chapters, a complete set of plans from one of my hikes is provided to show you how to record your planning information. Supplemental sections contain ready-reference information about post offices, services in Trail towns, climate and weather, calorie ratings for commonly used trail foods, and a product-guide section listing popular thru-hiker gear. A workbook section is located at the end of this book.

The ten planning chapters are the key to using this guide. Each covers everything necessary for planning one major segment of your hike, and you can begin using most chapters individually, without reference to the others. In practice, you will find yourself working on several chapters simultaneously, and some of the planning steps in various chapters will begin to overlap and mesh as your final plans come together. The order in which you begin using the chapters is up to you. Six chapters—Guidebooks and Maps, Equipment, Footwear, Clothing, Food and Supplies, and Health and Hygiene—involve plans that require actions (buying gear, choosing footwear, *etc.*) well before you begin your hike. You may want to start working on these chapters first. The remaining four chapters—Scheduling and Maildrops, Budgeting and Finances, Miscellaneous Topics, and Last-Minute Preparations—involve plans that will come to fruition mainly after you begin your hike, so you may want to briefly delay working on these chapters until you feel you have those in the first group under control. When you have worked your way through all ten chapters, your planning will be complete.

As you start using the individual chapters, you will notice that each has a discussion section with subheadings, and that most end with a section of planning steps. The purpose of each section is as follows:
• The discussion section shares general information about the chapter's topic in the context of an A.T. thru-hike, giving you an overview of the things past thru-hikers have found important. It points out things you should consider, and relates the range of options available to you as you make your plans.
• The planning-steps section lists the necessary steps for planning the segment of your hike discussed in the chapter, and can be used as a checklist. The steps lead you through your planning in a logical and systematic manner, though you may need to modify or add to them, or in some cases ignore a step, to fit your particular situation.

Each chapter will require you to gather information and make decisions about things you will use and do on your hike. You will need the information to assemble equipment, food, maildrop contents, and other physical components for use on the Trail. Systematically recording these planning details and decisions as you go along is essential, so that they can be easily retrieved. Planning forms used to record the details of one of my thru-hikes are referred to in the chapters, and these forms, which are printed on yellow paper and illustrated in the "Sample Planning Notebook" section that begins on page 59, will show you how to record your planning information in a concise and systematic manner. The workbook section at the end of this guide provides blank planning forms for your use as you plan the details of your hike.

Using a Planning Notebook

Most of the information needed to actually do your hike can be recorded on the planning forms in the workbook section of this guide. However, in the course of your planning, you may gather a lot of supplemental information (equipment brochures, comparative food prices at various stores, transportation prices and schedules, *etc.*) that will help you make wise planning decisions but will not be needed on your planning forms. A good way to keep this supplemental information organized and handy is to use a separate planning notebook, which is simply a standard three-ring binder with eight tabbed dividers, arranged and used as follows:
• Label the eight tabs, one each for Equipment, Clothing and Footwear, Food and Supplies, Hiking Schedule, Maildrops, Lodging, Budgeting and Finances, and Miscellaneous (or you may choose another arrangement more suitable to your own plans).
• File the supplemental information you gather behind the appropriate tabbed divider for easy future reference and recall. Also, you will often think of a question about one aspect of your planning while busy planning another, so you should form the habit of writing down your questions as soon as they arise (and before you

forget them) and filing them behind the appropriate tabbed divider for later attention.
- Place a sheet of paper labeled "Things to Do" in the front of your planning notebook and form the habit of immediately listing things that need to be done as soon as you think of them, no matter how obvious or mundane, then cross them out as you do them.

As indicated above, a complete set of plans for a thru-hike are illustrated in the "Sample Planning Notebook" section. Observe that all vital information needed for preparing and doing a thru-hike is contained on a relatively few pages of planning forms. The information is concise and easy to retrieve. By using this guide, its workbook section, and a supplemental planning notebook of your own, as outlined above, you will accomplish your planning efficiently. More important, you will complete your planning with the assurance that you have made all necessary preparations for doing your thru-hike.

As You Begin Planning, Remember ...

Your goal as you use this guide is not to discover "the ordained way" of doing a thru-hike and then conform your plans to it. Of the more than 2,800 people who have successfully hiked the entire Trail, no two have done it in exactly the same manner. Knowing this, feel free to plan a thru-hike that expresses your style and manner of doing things. Profit from the advice of others, but make your own decisions. Also keep in mind that you will not be thru-hiking for six uninterrupted months in the woods. Instead, you will be hiking about a weekl in the woods, staying a day or so in town, hiking another week in the woods, staying another day in town, and so on all the way to the end. Do not get sidetracked by trying to cope with two-thousand continuous miles of hiking. Think of your thru-hike as essentially a one-week hike repeated over and over, which it is, and make your plans accordingly.

1

Guidebooks and Maps

Thru-hikers carry a variety of publications with them on their hikes. Several of the more popular publications—guidebooks and maps intended primarily for on-Trail use—will be needed for doing planning before your hike as well. Specifically, they will be used when you start drafting your hiking schedule and picking your resupply points. The information in these guidebooks and maps, some or all of which you will choose to carry and use during your hike, has been intentionally omitted from this guide, so that, as you use these publications to do your planning, you will also become familiar with how to use them on the Trail.

The principal publications of interest to thru-hikers are listed below, and the features offered by each are described and illustrated. At the minimum, you will need the *A.T. Data Book* and *The Thru-hiker's Handbook*, both considered by past thru-hikers to be indispensable for both planning and hiking purposes. The latest editions of these two publications should be obtained right away. Together with this planning guide, they will give you all of the basic information needed for planning and doing your hike. The remaining publications contain valuable information, and many thru-hikers have found having them makes planning more thorough and doing a thru-hike more enjoyable. You will probably do your planning with the editions published for the year prior to your hike, which is usually fine, but the latest editions should be carried with you during your hike. If any of the publications below are unavailable through your local outfitter or bookstore, you can order them direct by calling the specific publisher listed for each publication.

A.T. Data Book

The *A.T Data Book* is a pocket-sized ready reference booklet showing mileage figures between major features along the entire Trail, with information shown both north to south and south to north. It is intended for making broad-scale plans but does not contain enough information for detailed planning. Features listed include shelters and official campsites, road crossings, major water sources, principal mountain peaks and gaps, and other notable landmarks. Locations of the closest post office, lodging, meals, and grocery stores at road crossings are also listed in coded form, with distance and direction from the Trail indicated, but no descriptive information about prices, hours, or other details is given. The *Data Book* is updated and published annually, with the latest edition normally available in late January. Size, 5-inches wide x 7-inches high (see full-size illustration on page 12); weight, 3.5 ounces. *Published by the Appalachian Trail Conference; $3.95 plus shipping and handling.*

The Thru-hiker's Handbook

The Thru-hiker's Handbook is a concise guide for doing end-to-end A.T. hikes, intended for detailed planning and designed to be carried and used on the Trail as you do your hike, with information shown south to north. It is especially useful because it provides specialized information about post offices, businesses, and services in towns and other locations along the entire Trail route from Georgia to Maine. Designed to be used as a companion to the *Data Book*, it gives "the inside scoop" (prices, days and hours, services offered, *etc.*) on hundreds of hiker-friendly hostels, motels, restaurants, grocery stores, laundromats, stove-fuel sources, cobblers, outfitters, and other services needed by thru-hikers. In addition, it contains useful information about shelters and water sources, and interesting tidbits about wildlife, wildflowers, history, and points of interest on or near the Trail. Maps of the most frequently used Trail towns and communities, showing locations of the most frequently used facilities, are included. The *Handbook* is updated and published annually, with the latest edition normally available in early January. Many past thru-hikers recommend that you buy two copies of the *Handbook*, one to carry with you, the other to leave with the folks back home, especially if they are providing your logistical support, so that they can have current information about the places you are visiting as you hike. Size, 5.5-inches wide x 8.5-inches high (see full-size illustration on page 13); weight, 8 ounces. *Published by the Center for Appalachian Trail Studies; $10.95 includes shipping and handling.*

10

A.T. Guidebooks and Maps

The *A.T. Guidebooks* are an eleven-volume set of pocket-sized guides describing the actual route of the footpath in detail, sometimes down to a tenth of a mile, with descriptions given both north to south and south to north. Each volume covers a substantial section of the A.T., with volumes divided as follows: Maine, New Hampshire and Vermont, Massachusetts and Connecticut, New York and New Jersey, Pennsylvania, Maryland and Northern Virginia, Shenandoah National Park, Central Virginia (south to the New River), Southwest Virginia (south of the New River), Tennessee and North Carolina (south to Davenport Gap), North Carolina (south of Davenport Gap) and Georgia. Each guidebook comes with a set of up to twelve durable topographic maps, with elevation profiles, showing the section described in the text. In addition, the *Guidebooks* include information on side trails, shelters and water sources, access points, history, and points of interest. Each volume is updated every two or three years. The eleven volumes are available individually or as a set. The maps, except those for Maine, can be purchased separately. Size (each volume), 4.5-inches wide x 7-inches high (see full-size illustrations on page 14); weight less maps, 4-8 ounces per volume. *Published by the Appalachian Trail Conference; $14.95-$19.95 per volume plus shipping and handling.*

In November, the ATC usually offers members a complete set of Guidebooks,
plus a copy of the Data Book, for about $110, plus shipping charges.

A.T. Poster Map

The *A.T. Poster Map* is a handsome four-color poster map of the Appalachian Trail (scale: 1 inch = 10 miles), valuable for giving you an overview of where places are located along the entire Trail route as you are planning, and an excellent item to wall mount so that the folks back home can follow your progress as you do your hike. Size, 32-inches wide x 48-inches high. *Published by the Appalachian Trail Conference; $2.95 plus shipping and handling.*

PLANNING STEPS - GUIDEBOOKS AND MAPS

Step 1. Purchase the *A.T. Data Book*, *The Thru-hiker's Handbook*, and any other on-Trail publications you want to use for planning or to carry on your hike.

Step 2. Write your name and home address on each publication and map you plan to carry with you on your hike, with instructions for mailing them back to you should you lose them.

Step 3. If you plan to carry the *Guidebook* maps, number all maps with your own numbers (in ascending order, either south-to-north or north-to-south) for quick identification of the next map to use during your hike.

North Carolina-Georgia

GBS	North to South	FEATURES	Facilities (See page xv for codes)	South to North	GBS
	Miles from Fontana Dam, N.C.		*Miles from Springer Mountain, Ga.*		
♦	0.0	Little Tennessee River, Fontana Dam Southern boundary, Great Smoky Mountains National Park	R	164.1	♦
N.C. 3	0.4	Fontana Dam Visitors Center (M,w on A.T.)	Mw	163.7	N.C. 3
	0.7	Fontana Dam Shelter	Sw	163.4	
	1.8	N.C. 28; **Fontana Dam, N.C., P.O. 28733** (P.O.,G,L,M 2m W)	RGLM	162.3	
	4.5	Walker Gap		159.6	
	5.9	Black Gum Gap		158.2	
	7.3	Cable Gap Shelter	Sw	156.8	
♦	8.2	Yellow Creek Gap, Yellow Creek Gap Road (L 5m E)	RL	155.9	♦
N.C. 4	10.6	Cody Gap	w	153.5	N.C. 4
	11.4	Hogback Gap		152.7	
	13.2	Brown Fork Gap	w	150.9	
	15.0	Sweetwater Gap		149.1	
♦	16.0	Stecoah Gap, Sweetwater Creek Road (N.C. 143)	Rw	148.1	♦
	18.1	Simp Gap		146.0	
	19.5	Locust Cove Gap	w	144.6	
N.C. 5	21.9	Cheoah Bald		142.2	N.C. 5
	23.1	Sassafras Gap Shelter	Sw	141.0	
	24.0	Swim Bald	Cw	140.1	
	26.9	Grassy Gap	w	137.2	
	28.4	Wright Gap		135.7	
♦	30.0	U.S. 19, Nantahala River; **Wesser, N.C.** (G,L,M on A.T.)	RGLM	134.1	♦
	30.8	A. Rufus Morgan Shelter	Sw	133.3	
N.C. 6	34.1	Jumpup Lookout		130.0	N.C. 6
	35.7	Wesser Creek Trail	C	128.4	
	35.8	Spring	w	128.3	
	36.5	Wesser Bald		127.6	

Appalachian Trail Data Book–1993   59

Illustration: *A.T. Data Book*

Copyright 1993 by Appalachian Trail Conference
(used by permission)

North Carolina-Tennessee

Silers Bald Shelter: side trail leads about 300 feet to spring. (5620') 1.7m→

Double Spring Gap Shelter: where a 1990 thru-hiker hung his food in a tree while he explored a side trail. A bear climbed the tree and started rocking it until the food bag swung close enough to be snared. The bear enjoyed five days of hiker food, the *piece de resistance* being a can of pressurized cheese that exploded in the bear's mouth. The hiker's comment, "It was a damn hungry bear." The bear replied with a cheesey grin. (5510') 6.3m→

Treeline is assumed to occur at 7,200 feet in the South, well above the highest summits in the Smokies, so it is impossible to go above treeline in this park. The evergreen line is quite evident, however. As you gain altitude through this section, notice the quick change from deciduous to mixed forest to totally evergreen forest above 5,800 feet.

Note—About a half mile south of Clingmans Dome, the A.T. bears left over a low ledge, while the more obvious footpath continues (in the same direction you have been walking) to the Clingmans Dome parking area. Watch the blazes carefully.

Clingmans Dome: at 6,643 feet, the highest point on the A.T. The summit is 0.1 mile off the Trail, topped by an observation deck with photos identifying the distant peaks and sights in all directions. Sightseers in city dress come up on a paved walkway from a parking/restroom area 0.5 mile below the summit. Most are unaware of the nearby A.T. and will often show real interest when they discover that you are hiking the Trail. Some will probably ask permission to take your picture. When someone says that it is "all downhill from here," do not believe them!

Mt. Collins Shelter: on side Sugarland Mountain Trail to the left; water available on this side trail about 100 yards past the shelter turnoff from a small spring on the right. A blue-blazed trail leads from the shelter to another water source, but this one is down a steep, obstacle-ridden trail. A composting privy was added last year. (5680') 7.5m→

Red wolves have been returned to GSMNP after an absence of nearly a century. Two pairs (four of only 135 genetically pure individuals alive) were released by the Fish and Wildlife Service in 1991, and two family groups are running free with pups in the Cades Cove and Tremont areas this year. Red wolves, which have tawny, cinnamon-colored fur, are extremely shy creatures that hunt for small mammals, such as piglets, usually alone and at night. It is hoped that 50 to 75 of these predators will inhabit the park and surrounding national forests by the end of the decade.

Newfound Gap (US441): *On A.T.*–parking area with restrooms and Rockefeller Memorial where President Franklin D. Roosevelt dedicated the park. *Left 14m*–to Great Smoky Mountain National Park HQ (704-498-2327); one mile farther to the town of Gatlinburg. *Right 21m*-to the town of Cherokee.

☏ GATLINBURG, TENN. (pop. 3,500): a full-fledged tourist mecca that overwhelms the senses after a few weeks in the woods; many motels and restaurants. A 25¢ shuttle bus runs continually during the day to all points mentioned below. **Lodging**—Willow Motel: $18S $20D $5EAP, 4 max; a/c, cable, pool, pets allowed (MC, Visa); owner Dennis Reagan welcomes hikers ▪ Grand Prix Motel: $26S $36D $2EAP, 4 max; a/c, cable, phone in room, use of refrigerator, pool, no pets (MC, Visa, AE, Dis). **Places to eat**—Ruby Tuesday: L/D, some

37

Illustration: *The Thru-hiker's Handbook*

Copyright 1994 by Dan Bruce

78   Appalachian Trail Guide to North Carolina-Georgia

Shelters, Campsites, and Water

Fontana Dam Shelter is located in the TVA complex at Fontana Dam. Cable Gap Shelter is 7.9 miles from the northern end of the section.

Water sources are infrequent, and in dry seasons even well-recognized sources may fail. Make ample provisions for water.

The USFS maintains the Horse Cove Campground, adjacent to the Joyce Kilmer Memorial Forest (see page 72). Camping is permitted in the Slickrock portion of the wilderness area.

Public Accommodations

Peppertree Fontana Village, two miles west of the A.T. on N.C. 28, is an excellent supply source, with a general store and post office. In Robbinsville, North Carolina, 8.6 miles west on Sweetwater Road, accommodations are available (by reservation) at the Snowbird Mountain Lodge.

Trail Description, North to South

Miles	Data
0.0	From the north bank of the Little Tennessee River, follow the roadway across the dam.
0.4	Reach the south bank. On the right at south abutment of dam are visitors' buildings with exhibits, a refreshment stand (closed in winter), restrooms, and public showers. Ascend on hard-surfaced road.
0.9	At ridgecrest, pass parking overlook on left, with good views of Fontana Lake to the Great Smokies, and a picnic area with water fountains, restrooms (closed in winter), and, 300 feet into the woods, the **Fontana Dam Shelter**. Descend on hard-surfaced road.
1.0	Bear left onto Trail into woods, continuing along curving ridgecrest, with gentle ascents and descents. Descend to hard-surfaced road at swimming pool, bear left, and cross

Illustration: *A.T. Guidebook* (map profile below)

Copyright 1989, 1990 by Appalachian Trail Conference
(used by permission)

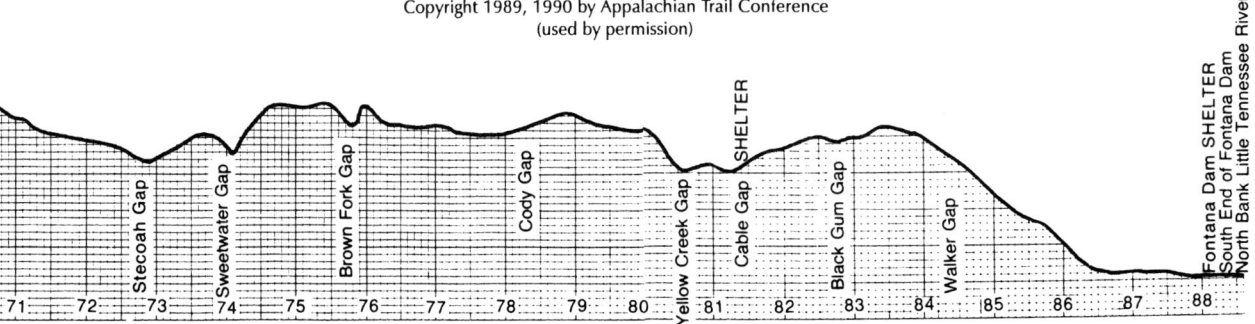

14

2

Equipment

Quite a few thru-hikers start their hikes with too much equipment or the wrong equipment, and they immediately regret it. The smart ones quickly learn that a lightweight pack makes them a happy hiker and send unnecessary items home. An unfortunate few are forced to reequip in mid-hike, which is both time consuming and expensive. Both inconveniences can be avoided by choosing your equipment wisely and starting your hike with only the equipment you need to function efficiently on the Trail. You will need equipment designed for three-season use (spring, summer, autumn) unless you are beginning or ending your hike very early or late in the year. Everest-style expedition gear is usually too complicated, cumbersome, and heavy for use on a thru-hike, as is gear intended primarily for car camping. When choosing the equipment for your hike, stick with items designed specifically for backpacking. As for quality, the equipment for doing a thru-hike is not radically different from that used for two-day or three-day hikes. The major difference is that weight and durability are more important. You will have to carry everything on your back for many days and many miles over many mountains, so the lighter weight the better. However, the gear you choose must also be durable enough to stand the rigors of a six-month journey in ever-changing conditions, and that sometimes means selecting something besides the lightest weight gear on the market. Price is also another major consideration for most thru-hikers. In general, you do get what you pay for, but, if your budget is tight, know that many thru-hikes have been done successfully and enjoyably with modestly priced gear.

Choosing Equipment

The first step in choosing the equipment to use on your thru- hike is to make a list of every item you think you will need for your hike. A sample equipment checklist is illustrated on page 60 to assist you. It lists the essential items needed to begin an A.T. thru-hike, based on a survey what many past thru-hikers have retained in their packs a few weeks after they have begun their hikes and had time to send unnecessary items home. Notice that items on the sample checklist are grouped by function (a backpack for carrying gear, a tent and groundsheet for shelter, a sleeping bag and pad for sleeping, and so on), and you should similarly plan your equipment list based on how you expect to function on the Trail. Once you have a list of equipment that satisfies you from the standpoint of function, compare the items on your list with the equipment you have on hand. This will tell you which equipment items you need to research and buy. Also notice that the sample checklist has space for recording the weight of each item, to help monitor total pack weight as equipment is being selected, and you should do the same as you select your gear.

If you do not plan to use an item every day, except for safety items (first-aid kit, rainwear, *etc.*) and a luxury item or two (paperback, Walkman, *etc.*), resist the urge to add it to your equipment list unless you know from experience that you will need it. You can always have those "favorite extras" sent to you later, when you have been on the Trail long enough to judge if they are really worth the additional weight. Also resist the urge to rush out and buy new gear without doing some consumer research. If time permits, shop around. Write or call for catalogues from manufacturers and distributors (see page 93 for addresses and telephone numbers). Visit the outfitters in your area, study their product lines, and get the opinions of their sales personnel. Consider the comments about gear in this guide, which, by the way, are not intended as a substitute for your own consumer research. Gather as much information as you can and use it to revise and refine your equipment list until you arrive at a combination "on paper" that meets your specific needs, including total pack weight, before you purchase any new equipment.

If you already have gear in good condition, and it has been working well for you on previous hiking excursions, consider using it on your hike. Do not buy new equipment just to be fashionable on the Trail. Some thru-hikers

15

make much ado about having the very latest gear, but most do not. If you have access to a sewing machine, you can even make some of your simpler gear, such as stuff sacks. Mail-order catalogues and many local outfitters sell coated-nylon cloth by the yard (or you can salvage usable cloth from worn-out items, such as raincovers), and a range of accessories is available. Besides being a lot of fun to make, homemade gear will be exactly the size you need, and you will often save money.

Buying Equipment

Chances are you will want to purchase new gear for your hike, just to be on the safe side. In selecting the individual pieces of equipment for a thru-hike, you will have to evaluate and balance many features, especially weight, durability, and price, realizing that few products are superior in all three categories. Of the three, weight may at first seem the most important for a thru-hike. Total pack weight is the critical factor, however, not the weight of any single item, so you have some leeway in selecting individual pieces of gear. Put your spending emphasis on the major items: boots, backpack, tent, sleeping bag, and stove. Keep in mind that most name-brand equipment items designed for long-distance use are suitable for a thru-hike (none are absolutely perfect), so pick good gear, but do not waste valuable planning time nitpicking over your choice of brands. After all, it will not be the label on your gear that will ultimately get you from Georgia to Maine or *vice versa*.

You will have three main sources for obtaining gear: mail-order catalogues, your local retail outfitters, and equipment manufacturers. The mail-order catalogues offer a large variety and may be slightly less expensive, even after you pay shipping charges, but you will have to wait a few weeks for delivery. You will also be dealing with a stranger over the telephone or by mail. Your local retail outfitter will usually (but not always) have less inventory than the mail-order catalogues, but you can see the equipment firsthand and make sure that it is exactly what you need before you buy. You also have the advantage of dealing face to face with a person, usually one who knows backpacking, and this personal service can be invaluable if you are new to backpacking or later have an equipment problem that requires warranty replacement on the Trail. Several manufacturers sell direct to the public, especially if they specialize in one category or item of gear, so, in some cases, you may be able to buy direct. Since even the best equipment can fail during a thru-hike, ask your equipment source about warranty procedures if you later have an equipment defect develop during your hike. Do this before you buy. Avoid products that require you to send them back to the manufacturer for inspection before warranty action is taken. During your hike, you cannot hang around a Trail town for a week or two waiting for a replacement.

Back-up Equipment

As you assemble the equipment for your trip, you will undoubtedly end up buying new gear to replace older items you have on hand. These older items become useful back-up equipment you can send for if needed during your hike. The best way to handle this is to pack all back-up items in paper or plastic bags, one item per bag, and number them. Next, make a list of the numbers and corresponding bagged items. Take a copy of the list with you and leave the numbered gear with the person who will be sending it to you. When you must call from the Trail for an item, ask for it by number. This method does not require your helper back home to be an equipment expert and virtually eliminates surprises at the post office (the wife of one thru-hiker, who requested his back-up boots, sent him two left boots!)..

Loading Your Pack

Once you have all equipment items (and clothing) for your hike on hand, load your pack to see how everything fits together. Follow the weight-distribution instructions supplied by the pack manufacturer. Make sure the pack is balanced from side to side. This is very important. For instance, do not place a tent on one side unless you balance it with equal weight on the other side. Try to have everything packed inside your pack or inside a nylon stuff sack strapped securely to the pack. Have a specific place for everything, making sure that you have easy access to emergency items (first-aid kit, knife, flashlight, rainwear, *etc.*). With your pack fully loaded, check to make sure that it rides comfortably, and, if not, make adjustments until it does. Finally, verify that your raincover is large enough to protect your fully-loaded pack.

The Big Question: How much should your loaded pack weigh when you begin your hike? The average range seen on the Trail is 25-35 pounds without food, perhaps a little heavier if you are young and/or strong or carrying a lot of cold-weather gear. Total pack weight with your largest food load (figure about two pounds of food per day for planning purposes) should never exceed one-third of your body weight. Small hikers, those weighing less than 110 pounds or so, will have to plan extra carefully to stay within this percentage, but should do so. If you are sharing equipment with a companion, the total weight of shared items can be proportioned (not halved) between you according to your body weights and relative strengths. Later in your hike, after you get into Trail shape, you will find that you can carry additional weight without strain, but not at the beginning.

Essential Equipment

The discussion sections that follow give general information about each equipment category considered essential for doing a thru-hike and, at the end, a few "optional essentials" are listed. Information about the specific brands and models of major equipment items most frequently used by recent A.T. thru-hikers, and about new models that should prove especially suitable for thru-hiking, is listed in the "Thru-hiker's Product Guide" section that begins on page 89.

Backpack

Backpacks come in many sizes and shapes, but the first choice you must make for your hike is whether to use an internal-frame or external-frame pack. Each type has its advantages and disadvantages, so the right type for you will depend on which combination of features you prefer. Both types are used successfully for thru-hiking the A.T., with thru-hiker preference being about equally divided between the two types.

Internal-frame packs: Thru-hikers who use internals claim that they are more stable and feel more secure while hiking since they ride close to the body, and most hikers agree that the narrower construction gives better freedom of movement to the upper body in steep or rough terrain. Internals are easy to handle when traveling by vehicle, but, on older top-loading models, more inconvenient than externals to use during rest breaks and in crowded shelters since everything is carried in one large top-loading compartment, meaning you have to practically unload the contents to get to whatever it is you need. This is especially true with sleeping gear, normally carried in the bottom on most internal models, although newer models have a separate sleeping-bag compartment with zippered access. Many newer models now offer zippered access to main compartments, thus allowing you to easily retrieve gear from almost any location in the pack without unloading everything, and most models offer permanent or add-on outside pockets for carrying frequently used items. Since internal-frame packs hug the back and retain body heat, many thru-hikers have found this to be a source of discomfort in hot weather. Several manufacturers offer optional ventilated backpads to minimize overheating (some offer this feature as standard equipment), and you should probably buy one of these special backpacks for summer use if available on your model.

External-frame packs: Thru-hikers who use externals claim they are easy to load and balance, and feel that they offer more hiking stability because they more firmly hold the pack weight in the correct position over your center of gravity. They can efficiently transfer most of the pack weight to the hip area through the frame, thus substantially reducing upper-body fatigue by relieving strap pressure and weight on the shoulders. Externals come in both top-loading and panel-loading models (some models offer a combination of the two styles) and are available with either flexible or rigid frames. They are convenient to use in shelters (simply hang them on a nail or prop them in a corner and use the compartments and pockets as you would a chest of drawers), but can be awkward to handle when getting in and out of vehicles or tents with small openings. Many thru-hikers like the models that have pack bags with plenty of outside pockets, giving easy access to gear while hiking and while functioning in camp. Another feature liked by thru-hikers is the detachability of pack bags, straps, and belts from the frame, allowing machine washing when these items begin to reek from hundreds of miles of sweat. Just about everyone agrees that externals are cooler in hot weather because the frame holds the pack bag away from the torso and allows air to circulate on the back.

With both internals and externals, fit is crucial on a thru-hike. Most thru-hikers who change backpacks in mid-hike do so, not because there is anything wrong with the pack design, but because their pack does not fit them properly. If you are using an internal-frame pack, make sure that it is sized to your torso and that the internal supports will bend to fit the contour of your back. If using an external-frame pack, make sure that the frame is the proper length for your height and is adjusted to your torso. Several manufacturers offer backpacks proportioned for the female anatomy (shorter frame, slightly wider in the hip area, *etc.*), although most women thru-hikers use the same models as men and do so without problems if fitted properly. With either type, make sure the waist belt can be drawn tight and can be tightened more later, after you have lost your excess body fat. Most external-frame packs are offered with a choice of several belt sizes, usually ranging from 26 inches to 34 inches. Many outfitters display only the larger sizes, so you may have to request a smaller belt. You may even want to consider buying a belt slightly smaller than your prehike waist measurement, especially if you are overweight, or consider buying two belts so that you can send for the smaller one later. Internal-frame packs usually have the belt sewn to the pack bag, which does not allow you to change belts, so be extra careful that the pack you choose has a belt that will fit the "skinny" you later in your hike. Some of the newest internal-frame models now offer changeable belts in several sizes.

As for the pack volume required, that will depend on the bulkiness of your equipment, the amount of food you plan to carry between resupply stops, and the type of pack you choose. Everything is carried inside an internal-frame pack, whereas major items (sleeping bag, tent, *etc.*) are usually strapped outside the pack bag on externals. Consequently, you will need a larger volume internal-frame than external-frame pack for the same amount of gear. Also, keep in mind that the pack volume you will need for the majority of your hike (during the warmer months when you will be carrying bulky cold-weather clothing and larger daily food requirements) will be less than you need when you start your hike, so do not overestimate the volume you will need. It is easier to strap extra items on the outside of your pack at the beginning than it is to carry a half-empty pack later. Most thru-hikers use an external-frame pack with a volume between 3,800 and 5,500 cubic inches, and those using internals usually look for a pack that has between 4,500 and 6,000 cubic inches of carrying capacity.

A separate pack raincover is a necessity since no pack is waterproof on the A.T. in a driving rain, no matter what claims are made by the manufacturer. Be sure your raincover is large enough to fit over and around your fully-loaded pack (including your largest food load), and verify that the raincover has some system for fastening it securely to the pack in case of strong winds, which can strip away a raincover in an instant.

Tent

The A.T. has an extensive shelter system, with shelters usually spaced less than a moderate hiking-day's distance apart, but you should still carry a tent—or at least a tarp—for use in the event a shelter is full on a stormy night (a definite possibility for northbounders starting in March or April) or in case of an emergency. You will also find a tent useful for protection from insects on occasion, and having your own shelter will give you the freedom to camp between Trail shelters when you wish to make additional miles or have some solitude. The type of tent used by thru-hikers varies widely. A few use small bivy tents, accepting the limitations of space and figuring that they and/or their gear will possibly get wet a time or two. Others use large expedition models, often with many bells and whistles, and they stay dry and have plenty of space in camp but suffer from the additional weight while hiking. Most thru-hikers choose something in between that provides good protection from the elements and sufficient space for them and their gear at an acceptable weight.

Both free-standing and staked tents work equally well on a thru-hike, though a free-standing tent can be more easily moved to another spot if you discover your first tent site is less than ideal (hidden rocks and roots, bad slope, *etc.*). A free-standing tent is also easier to keep clean, because you can simply pick it up by the poles and shake out the dirt, and is easier to dry when wet. Most backpacking tents have a separate rain fly made of coated-nylon fabric, and these usually require some staking even on free-standing models. When choosing a tent, try to keep the weight below five or six pounds for one person, below three or four pounds per person if sharing. Make sure your tent has adequate ventilation, which, for a three-season tent, is usually proportional to the amount of no-see-um netting. Check to see that it has enough room for you and any companion to sit up comfortably and pack gear inside during a driving rain. Finally, verify that it is easy to set up in the dark (practice this before you start your hike), and consider that you may be setting up camp in blowing rain or wind on several occasions during your hike. Whichever type tent you use, make sure you seal the seams in accordance with the manufacturer's instructions. Also, check the stuff sack. Trying to put a wet tent into a tight-fitting stuff sack can be annoying, so you may want to substitute a slightly larger one.

Sleeping Bag

The problem with selecting a sleeping bag to use on an end-to-end A.T. hike is that the weather is usually cold on each end of your trip and hot and humid in the middle part. The best solution is to have two sleeping bags and carry the bag appropriate for the type of weather you anticipate having. A good combination is to have a cold-weather bag rated somewhere between 0-25°F., the low temperature being determined by how early you start or how late you end your thru-hike, and a summer bag rated between 30-55°F. If you are limited to one bag, choose the bag for cold weather. You can always use it unzipped as a blanket or sleep on top on hot nights.

Most thru-hikers use a mummy or modified-mummy bag, to save weight. Try to stay under four or five pounds for a cold-weather bag, under two or three pounds for a summer bag. Features that have proven important to thru-hikers are compressibility (How small does it pack?), roominess (Does it feel like a straight jacket?), and ventilation (How well does it breath and does the liner material feel clammy?). Other points you will want to consider are the area around the head opening (Can it be easily adjusted from inside the bag?), the zipper (Is it easy to operate from both inside and outside the bag?), and the draft tube that covers the zipper (Is it sufficient to stop drafts?). Bags come in regular and long lengths. If you are buying a new bag, do not purchase a long model if you do not need the extra length, which also means extra weight.

Of course, no sleeping bag generates warmth of its own but insulates by holding the warmth you generate close to your body. Both down and synthetic bags insulate well and are equally suitable for use on a thru-hike. Some points to consider when choosing which to use are discussed below:

Down bags: These bags will weigh less for a given temperature rating and give superior insulation per pound of weight, but down bags will cost more and be harder to wash on the Trail. Down is also useless as insulation when it gets wet, but this is not a problem on the A.T. unless you are careless, and many down bags come with a water-resistant or waterproof shell that deters moisture. Down bags with 550-fill-power down offer good loft; 650-fill-power (or greater) down is the fluffiest and warmest you can buy.

Synthetic bags: These bags will usually cost less, take more punishment, and be easier to wash and dry in Trail towns, but they are slightly heavier and bulkier for a given temperature rating compared to down. They are also stiffer than down bags, and thus do not wrap around the body as readily, although newer models with the latest synthetic materials come close to the feel of down bags. Most brand-name synthetic bags use quality fill materials suitable for a thru-hike. Some of the more popular fill materials among thru-hikers are Quallofil, Hollofil II, Polarguard, Lamilite, LiteLoft, Primaloft, and Micro-loft.

Whichever type bag you choose, synthetic or down, plan to carry it enclosed in a heavy-duty plastic garbage bag, with both sleeping bag and plastic bag carried inside a protective nylon stuff sack, the idea being to always have a dry sleeping bag to slip into in an emergency. If you sleep on your stomach most of the time, be sure to get a bag that is long enough when you stretch out, and good luck in very cold weather when you have to fully cinch the head opening to stay warm. (When is somebody going to offer a winter bag that is designed for us stomach-sleepers?) If you and a companion intend to zip bags together, make sure the zippers mate.

Sleeping Pad

A pad under you while you sleep is a necessity, not only for cushioning but to insulate you from cold and dampness. Even in warm weather, this is important. Two types of pads are seen on the Trail. The closed-cell (meaning it will not absorb water) foam pad is lightweight and inexpensive. The self-inflating pad (Therm·A·Rest brand is used almost exclusively on the A.T.) is more expensive and slightly heavier, but it packs smaller and is considered more comfortable and durable by most thru-hikers. Unless you are a heavyweight, the 1-inch-thick self-inflating pad is more than sufficient and weighs considerably less than the 1½-inch-thick model. Weight can also be saved by using a 3/4-length pad, but many thru-hikers appreciate a full-length pad because it cushions the upper body as well as their often sore ankles and feet. Both closed-cell foam and self-inflating pads should be carried in a protective nylon sack. *Hint*: Special lightweight slings are available that will convert a self-inflating pad to a fairly comfortable camp chair.

Groundcloth

A groundcloth should be carried for use under your tent, to prevent clamminess and protect the tent floor from dirt and abrasion. It can be made of inexpensive plastic sheeting, which will eventually puncture and may need to be replaced periodically. In rainy weather, this item will often stay wet and dirty, so quite a few hikers carry a second groundcloth as well, often a small nylon tarp or space blanket, to use under their sleeping gear in shelters, the floors of which can be very muddy from the residue left by wet hiker boots. If you have a second groundcloth, it can be used inside your tent to prevent wearing away the waterproof coating on the tent floor.

Stove

Few thru-hikers depend on campfires for cooking. If you have ever tried to start a fire with wet wood in pouring rain, or arrived in camp dead-tired and hungry after dark, you understand why they carry a stove. Many types of stoves are available, and your choice will be determined by your cooking requirements. If you plan to do a lot of cooking, you will need to look for high heat output and good fuel economy. You will also need a stove that simmers well. If you plan to only boil water once or twice a day, almost any type of stove will do. In either case, your stove should be easy to set up and should have good stability with your largest pot. Eating spilled food off the ground is no fun. When considering a stove for your hike, you will have two main fuel choices to consider, butane and Coleman-type white-gas, but stoves using other fuels have also appeared and been used successfully on the A.T. in recent years:

Butane stoves: Butane stoves burn clean, are easy to start and restart (they need no priming), and are generally lightweight, but have greatly decreased efficiency at higher altitudes and may be hard to start in very cold weather. Iso-butane mixes solve the latter problem. Butane fuel canisters are relatively expensive, though, and hard or impossible to find in many Trail towns along the A.T. Unfortunately, mailing them in maildrop packages is against postal regulations. Because of the uncertainty of fuel sources, few thru-hikers rely on butane stoves for their end-to-end hikes.

White-gas stoves: White-gas stoves often burn a little dirty and are usually heavier than butane stoves, but they put out a lot of heat and are the most fuel-efficient. Most models need priming to start and restart, a very minor inconvenience once you get the hang of it. Many white-gas stoves are designed to burn a variety of other petroleum-based fuels, most notably kerosene. This is a useful feature in other hiking areas, but no real advantage on a thru-hike because of the ready availability of Coleman-type fuel, which can be purchased in most Trail towns by the pint (a fill-up costs about $1; locations are listed in the *Handbook*). The majority of thru-hikers use some type of white-gas stove for their hikes.

Alcohol stoves: Alcohol stoves are beginning to appear more frequently on the A.T. They have the advantage of simplicity (no moving parts) and quietness, and need no priming. They also burn clean, without producing sooty pots and pans, and most models have superior stability. The newer models are almost as fuel-efficient as white-gas stoves. Denatured alcohol for these stoves can be obtained at most hardware stores along the Trail, and any automotive-parts store carries "dry gas" (pure methanol with coloring) by the pint. Shellac thinner is usually pure methanol and may also be used. European thru-hikers should note that methylated spirits is called *denatured alcohol* in the U.S. In hot weather, add a little water to your alcohol fuel to reduce the high burning temperature and prolong fuel use.

Equipment

Wood-burning stoves: Wood-burning stoves are just beginning to appear on the Trail. These backpacking stoves have the advantage of requiring you to carry no fuel, since you use wood scraps and charred wood found along the Trail and in fire pits (some thru-hikers have even used their burnable garbage as fuel). They put out a lot of heat, and also put out smoke (but no more than a small campfire, and a feature which is often welcome on a buggy night). Pots and pans stay sooty, so you will need a bag for carrying your cooking gear. Users of these stoves should also carry a small Ziploc-type bag of dry kindling or fire-starter for "priming" during rainy periods, when dry starter wood is sometimes difficult to find.

Whichever stove you choose, cook with it at home (outside, of course ... and never cook inside your tent!), to make sure it works and to test its fuel consumption per meal. This will give you some idea of the size fuel bottle you will need on your hike. Most thru-hikers take a one-quart fuel bottle if they cook a lot, a one-pint bottle if they cook less. Use only plastic or metal containers designed for carrying fuel, since other types may leak in your pack and damage your gear. Note that alcohol requires an anodized aluminum bottle. A pour spout makes refilling your stove easier, safer, and less wasteful.

Cookset

The pots and pans used by thru-hikers show more personality than any other equipment category. Some hikers use clever nesting sets made especially for backpacking. Others assemble odds and ends from their kitchen at home. Either way is fine. The important thing is to have enough cooking volume for your largest meal without having any unnecessary weight. If cooking for one person, you will need at least a one-quart pot and lid. A one-pint pot will also prove useful, but no lid is needed for the smaller pot. If sharing meals with a partner, larger cooking vessels will be needed. You can experiment at home, using kitchen utensils to cook a few Trail meals, to determine the size pots you will need before you purchase a cookset. Include a nonstick frying pan if you want to cook edible pancakes or stir-fry. Good breads (and even complete meals) are possible with a BakePacker. Several funnel-shaped contraptions now on the market allow you to make excellent brewed coffee. A drinking cup with liquid-measurement scale is handy, especially if you are using freeze-dried foods which require exact water quantities for proper reconstitution. Some type of scouring pad should be carried in your cookset, because you will no doubt scorch a meal now and then. *Hint*: Carry an 8-inch-square piece of plastic mesh, the kind used to bag fruit or onions, which weighs nothing, drys quickly, and does not retain food particles that develop foul smells.

Utensils

A metal spoon and knife are the only utensils carried by most thru-hikers. Some add a fork if they include a frying pan in their cookset. More exotic Trail cooks carry miniature backpacking spatulas and whisks. Many thru-hikers recommend that you stay away from plastic utensils, which can melt and bend into interesting but unusable shapes while cooking or become brittle and break in cold temperatures. However, if you do choose to use lightweight plastic utensils, carry spares. See knife discussion below.

Butane Lighter

A butane lighter is easier to use and more dependable than matches, although it is wise to have a stash of preferably waterproof matches stored in your cookset (in a plastic bag) as a back-up fire-starter in case your lighter malfunctions. *Hint*: Buy only clear-plastic lighters, so that you can always see how much fuel you have left. Also, note that you can still sometimes start a petroleum-fuel or alcohol stove with the spark from a lighter, even if the fuel is spent.

Water Bottles and Bag

The amount of water you carry while hiking will depend on your metabolism and the heat and humidity along the Trail as the year progresses. Some hikers drink large quantities of water. Others seem to drink hardly any water as they hike along and only small quantities during breaks. If you do not know your water requirement from past hiking experience, start your hike with two water bottles, one each of the one-quart and one-pint sizes (wide-mouth types are easier to use with drink mixes; the Nalgene brand is used almost exclusively by thru-hikers). This should be enough volume to hold you between water sources. A water bag, with plastic bladder and on-off spout, is the best way to avoid extra trips to shelter water sources, some of which, at the end of a long hiking day, are located a seemingly never-ending distance from the shelter. A water bag can also be used to carry water in your pack for several miles if you wish to camp away from a convenient water source. Plastic soft-drink bottles picked up in town can be used to temporarily increase your water-carrying capacity while hiking through water-scarce sections if you feel the need during your hike.

Water Purifier

Water is fairly abundant on the Trail. Each day you will usually pass half a dozen or more springs or streams suitable for use as water sources, except in some water-scarce sections noted in the various guidebooks. In practice, most thru-hikers tend to drink from these springs, and from streams flowing from protected watersheds, without purifying. This is a calculated risk on their part, since none of the open water sources along the Trail are guaranteed safe, even those at shelters. To be absolutely safe, the accepted advice is that you should boil or treat all water used for drinking, cooking, and cleaning, including that used for bathing and brushing teeth. Boiling is impractical as a purification method for the average thru-hiker, however, because of the large amount of fuel and cooling time required. That leaves treating, which means using chemical purifiers or filters.

Chemical purifiers: Chemical purifiers usually use chlorine—some hikers use household bleach—or iodine to kill organisms. Most of the more popular brands (Potable Aqua and PolarPure) use iodine, either in tablet or saturated-liquid form. They are fairly easy to use and very inexpensive per gallon purified. Some hikers do not like the "medicine taste" of chemical purifiers, and none are recommended for use day after day.

Filters: Filters with pumps are used by most thru-hikers for purifying their water. The prices and weights of these devices vary greatly, as do the filtering characteristics and ease of use. Some models remove not only organisms but chemical impurities as well. Make sure that any filter you consider removes the *giardia lamblia* cyst. Also pay attention to the volume of water that can be filtered before a replacement filter is needed, keeping in mind that the manufacturer's figures are probably based on tests that use water with less sediment than that found on the A.T., and check the ease of cleaning both filter and pump. In practice, thru-hikers who depend on filters do not use them every day. They normally use them about one day of every three or four days they spend on the Trail, filtering about 4-6 quarts of water per day when they filter.

Kits

The numerous small items needed on a thru-hike can be divided by function into kits. Components of each kit are best stored together in a stuff sack or Ziploc-type plastic bag for easy retrieval from your pack. You will need a first-aid kit, a grooming kit, and a toilet kit. You may also want to have a miscellaneous/repair kit for storing those odds and ends that are necessary to keep your equipment functioning on the Trail, and a sewing kit is a must for doing on-the-spot repairs. A sample kits checklist is illustrated on page 61, and the components carried by most thru-hikers are listed below.

First-aid kit: aspirin or equivalent, antibiotic ointment, fungicide, powder (for chafing), antacid tablets, lip balm, a few Band-aids (for cuts, not blisters), roll of 1-inch-wide gauze, 2x2-inch sterile pads, large sterile pad, surgical tape, 2-inch-wide Ace bandage, and moleskin or equivalent. Optional items include allergy pills, cortisone cream, sunscreen, eye drops, toothache medicine, diarrhea medicine, Second Skin, scissors, tweezers, and snakebite kit. Many thru-hikers carry insect repellent, made from natural or man-made ingredients, with those containing DEET being the most frequently seen. Some also carry Avon Skin-So-Soft bath oil, which seems to repel no-see-ums. (See first-aid discussion on page 40.)

Grooming kit: toothbrush, toothpaste, floss, biodegradable soap, comb or brush, and nail clippers. Optional items include deodorant, razor, mirror, wash cloth, and towel. The new synthetic-chamois pack towel is considered a useful item by many thru-hikers. (See grooming discussion on page 42.)

Equipment

Toilet kit: toilet paper and matches (in plastic bag). Optional items include a plastic trowel for digging cat holes (most thru-hikers just use their boot heels) and feminine hygiene items.

Miscellaneous/repair kit: spare parts for pack and stove, Therm·A·Rest repair kit, extra flashlight bulbs and batteries, boot glue, and boot waterproofing.

Sewing kit: large-eye needles, top-stitching thread, and a thimble. Optional items include regular threads (wrapped around a piece of cardboard to save weight) to match the colors of your clothing, and regular darning needles.

Knife
A knife is needed only for food preparation and gear maintenance, so these uses should determine the type of knife you select for your trip. Most thru-hikers choose a Swiss Army knife with a variety of specialized blades and gizmos. You will need a good cutting blade and a can opener for food preparation, and a screwdriver and auger for doing maintenance on boots and pack. Some hikers swear by the scissors feature, and others are just as convinced that the corkscrew is a necessity. A few thru-hikers carry models which could probably be used to perform an appendectomy, but the extra weight of these impressive but useless gadgets is unjustifiable. Keep your knife simple and lightweight.

Light Sources
You will use a flashlight very little during most of your hike (it doesn't get dark until about 9:30 p.m. in midsummer), but your life may depend on it in an emergency, so choose a good one. The types most often used on the A.T. are waterproof and built to take abuse. A spare bulb and an extra set of batteries, which can be the ones in your radio if it uses the same size batteries, should be standard accessories. You should consider attaching your flashlight to a loop of cord, so that it can be hung around your neck when you leave a shelter to "visit the woods" during the night, minimizing the chances of dropping it and leaving your hands free to do more important things. If you are the type that arrives late in camp, you may want to consider using a headlamp instead of a hand-held flashlight, so your hands can be free to prepare supper and lay out gear after dark. If you plan to read a book or write in your journal after dark, include a candle lantern, or at least a candle, in your gear. This will conserve battery power and disturb other hikers less. Brands of flashlights and headlamps frequently seen on the A.T. include MagLite, TeknaLite, Panasonic, Petzl, and REI.

Compass and Whistle
You will probably never have to use either your compass or whistle for emergency purposes. Nevertheless, you should carry both with you at all times in the woods. The compass you choose can be basic but should be rugged and dependable. Equally important, you should know how to use it. If your compass does not come with instructions, check your library for a book or video on navigation. The whistle can be the inexpensive kind made of plastic. The reason for carrying a whistle is to allow you to call for help with a minimum of effort. You can blow a whistle a lot longer than you can yell, and it makes noise that carries farther. Three short blasts signal distress, two indicate response.

Rope and Cord
Rope is not necessary on a thru-hike, but you will need lightweight nylon parachute-type cord (about the same diameter as your boot laces) for hanging your food bag and as a clothes line. A 50-foot length should be more than sufficient, unless you are using a tarp for shelter. Melt the ends of the cord with a butane lighter or match to keep your cord from unraveling. Emergency boot laces can be cut from this cord as needed.

Datapouch
Quite a bit of information must be carried along on an A.T. thru-hike. The specifics will vary, but many thru-hikers carry a *Data Book*, *Handbook*, *Guidebooks*, maps, journal, address book, copy of their hiking schedule,

postcards, nature guides or finders, and a pen or two. You should keep all of these items in a large Ziploc-type bag and/or a zippered nylon pouch for quick reference and for protection from the elements. You will also find it very useful to have all of this data, plus your wallet, together in one pouch when you are going to the post office, making telephone calls, and doing other chores in towns.

Sitting Pad (opt.)

A sitting pad is useful when you take a break or stop for lunch, especially after you lose your body fat and it is bone against rock every time you sit down, or in wet weather when the ground is saturated. A sitting pad can be made by cutting a 12-inch by 14-inch section from an old foam pad. Therm·A·Rest offers a self-inflating sitting pad, made to pack compactly like their larger self-inflating sleeping pads.

Radio/Tape Player (opt.)

Many thru-hikers consider these items out of place in the woods, but just as many would not be without them. If you do decide to carry one or both, limit your listening to earphones. You will be able to receive FM-stereo stations everywhere on the Trail (except Wesser, North Carolina). In addition to its entertainment value, a radio is a useful source of accurate weather information. As for listening while hiking, keep in mind that your best defense against a rattlesnake is the noise it makes. Portable television sets and cellular telephones are definitely out of place on the A.T., so leave them at home.

Hiking Stick (opt.)

A hiking stick is not a necessity for hiking the A.T., but many thru-hikers carry one because they find it so useful. Some even use two. On a rainy night in a shelter many years ago, a group of thru-hikers made a list of more than 200 ways in which a hiking stick could prove useful. Some of the uses: balance while hiking, fending off dogs, finding hidden stepping stones in muddy areas, clearing weeds, propping up a pack during rest breaks, leaning on while talking to someone in the middle of the Trail, hanging clothes during breaks, *etc*. A number of companies make both wooden and metal models, some telescoping for easy travel (*Tracks* by Cascade Design and the Leki *Super Makalu* are the two most popular models). An old ski pole makes an inexpensive hiking stick. Do not count on finding a good hiking stick among the deadwood in the woods. Few thru-hikers do. Under no circumstances should you even think of cutting a living sapling! *Hint:* Place your name and telephone number on your hiking stick. Many thru-hikers each year leave their sticks in cars when hitching in and out of town.

Binoculars (opt.)

Binoculars are used very little by thru-hikers once they are on the Trail. Most people find them to be just something else to hassle with, and the weight of even a lightweight pair is hard to justify for carrying day after day. The exception is for bird watching. If you are really into bird identification, then binoculars are a must.

Sunglasses (opt.)

Many thru-hikers think that they will be wearing sunglasses every day of their hike, but such is never the case. As soon as trees start to put out leaves, the Trail is mostly in shade, often being referred to as "the long, green tunnel" by those who go the distance. Sunglasses are quickly sent home. Prescription glasses, on the other hand, are another story. They are not optional for many people. If you only need reading glasses, you may want to find an inexpensive pair of plastic "drugstore" glasses that will be of no great loss if damaged or lost. If your visual needs are more complicated, you may want to have a nonbreakable pair of prescription glasses special-made for use during your trip. If you must hike in glasses, know that it can be a bother during rainy days or hot periods when you sweat a lot. Fogged lenses have caused more than a few thru-hikers to swear under their breaths, which usually only adds to the fogging problem. No one has found a good solution. Consider carrying an extra bandanna or cloth for cleaning your glasses frequently. Contact lenses are used and cared for on the Trail in the same manner as at home, but do not depend on spring water (which has sediment) for cleaning them. Carry a small container of cleaning solution.

Equipment Failure

Hiking day after day will put your equipment to the test, so occasional equipment failure is something you should expect. Some common failures experienced by past thru-hikers are broken pack straps or frames, punctured sleeping pads, stripped zippers (especially on packs and sleeping bags), clogged stove orifices, and malfunctioning water-filter pumps. Usually you will have some advance warning of equipment failure, especially if you form the habit of inspecting and maintaining you gear at each town stop. If you do experience a failure, handling the problem on the Trail is a hassle but not the major difficulty you may think, since you are never too far from help on the A.T. If something does break or show signs of failure during your hike, you have several options:

- Make on-the-spot repairs, using your sewing kit to mend broken pack straps, for instance, or using the repair kit recommended by the manufacturer if you have included it in your gear.
- Contact the outfitter who sold you the gear when you reach a telephone, requesting warranty repair or replacement. If you are not dealing with your local outfitter, you will have to explain that you are a thru-hiker and cannot wait for regular warranty procedures. You should also insist that replacement gear be overnight mailed to a post office, not shipped UPS or FedEx, since post offices by law cannot accept such private-carrier shipments.
- Purchase new gear from one of the outfitters near the Trail, or ask for a replacement from them (but only if they are a warranty representative for your equipment brand). Many Trail outfitters offer repair services for a wide range of equipment and have helped many past thru-hikers continue their hikes without major interruption.

PLANNING STEPS - EQUIPMENT

Step 1. Make a list of every piece of equipment you think you will need for doing your thru-hike, using the sample equipment and kits checklists shown on pages 60-61 as a guide.

Step 2. Inventory the equipment items you already have on hand and want to use on your hike.

Step 3. Compare the two lists to reveal which items you must buy before you start your hike.

Step 4. Gather as much information as you can about the items you must buy before you make any new equipment purchases. Visit your local outfitters, and request catalogues from manufacturers and distributors (see page 93 for addresses and telephone numbers).

Step 5. Work with your equipment list "on paper" until you have the ideal equipment combination for starting your hike. Verify that your total pack weight is within the suggested range.

Step 6. Purchase the gear for your trip, checking on warranty procedures before you make final purchases.

Step 7. Load your pack with all equipment items necessary for starting your hike. Verify that everything is balanced and secure, and that emergency items are easily accessed.

Step 8. Verify that your pack raincover will fit over your fully-loaded pack (including your largest food load).

Step 9. Make a list of back-up equipment, numbering and listing items as described in the discussion section. Go over mailing procedures with your helper who will mail back-up gear to you should you need it, and make a copy of your back-up gear list for carrying with you on the Trail.

3

Footwear

Past thru-hiker's consider footwear, which means boots and socks considered as a unit, to be their most important category of gear. This will be true for you, too, since you will not be able to continue your hike if you cannot maintain your feet in good condition. Footwear also affects other parts of your body, such as knee joints and leg muscles, and even hip joints and spine, so careful consideration should be given to choosing the boots and socks you will use to begin your hike. You should assume that you will need at least two pairs of boots during your hike. This assumption does not mean that you must purchase two pairs before you start, but it does mean that you should be prepared to obtain a second pair somewhere along the way if the first pair wears out or fails.

Choosing Boots

Prospective thru-hikers often ask past thru-hikers which is the best boot to use on an end-to-end hike. There is no good answer to that question. Since there are as many variations in feet as there are hikers, no one boot brand or model works for every thru-hiker. Your choice will be determined by your hiking characteristics and will be based on the shape of your feet, strength of your arches and ankles, total body and pack weight, and other such factors. If you are like most thru-hikers, the type of boot you select will be determined by your wallet, and to a lesser extent fashion, as much as anything else, but arch and ankle support, durability, comfort, and weight are more important on a thru-hike. For example, each extra pound on the feet is equivalent to five extra pounds on the back in the amount of effort you exert while hiking.

Types of Boots

Four main types of boots are used by thru-hikers, with all four types suitable for doing an end-to-end hike, depending on the user. Not every type will be suitable for every hiker, however, and you are probably the only person who can determine which type is right for you. You can narrow your options by considering the following descriptions and focusing on the type of boot that seems to best fit your particular needs. Brands and models of boots frequently used on the A.T. are listed in the "Thru-hiker's Product Guide" section that begins on page 89.

Lightweight fabric-leather boots: These boots usually weigh about 18-20 ounces per pair and often resemble sneakers but have more built-in support and a tread suitable for hiking. Most models are low-cut like sneakers. All models are fairly flexible and thus give only moderate arch support and no ankle support, but allow good foot and ankle flexibility, which allows you to get a feel for the lay of the Trail underfoot. Few models are waterproof because of their low cut. Hikers who choose to use these lightweight boots realize that they will need several pairs, possibly four or five, for a thru-hike. Thru-hikers have been getting about 400-500 miles of use per pair before the structural integrity begins to fail.

Medium-weight fabric-leather boots: These boots are similar in appearance to the lightweight boots, but weigh about 1½ to 3 pounds per pair and have higher tops. Because of the added materials used in these medium-weight boots, they have fairly good arch and ankle support, rivaling some all-leather models. They also have stiffer soles (usually glued to the uppers) giving more protection from rocks and roots. Few models are waterproof unless they have a Gore-Tex or similar nonporous liner. Medium-weight fabric-leather boots are not usually as durable as all-leather boots, but thru-hikers have been getting 800-1,200 miles of use per pair, and on some occasions as much as 1,500 miles per pair.

Medium-weight leather boots: These boots usually weigh 2½ to 4½ pounds per pair. They are not as flexible as the fabric-leather types but give more arch and ankle support. The all-leather construction offers more protection from water, even without a nonporous liner. All-leather boots require slightly more break-in time, but often have the advantage of being more easily repaired by cobblers along the Trail. Several methods of attaching the sole are used. Some boots have a molded sole glued to the leather uppers. Others use leather uppers stitched to a midsole, either inside or outside, with a Vibram-type lug sole glued to the mid-sole. Novice hikers like to debate the merits of each construction method, but veteran hikers will tell you that most popular brand-name leather hiking boots are suitably constructed for use on the A.T. Some models have waterproof Gore-Tex liners. Leather boots are durable, and thru-hikers have been regularly getting 1,200-1,800 miles of use per pair before new soles are needed, occasionally going all the way in a single pair.

Heavyweight leather boots: These boots often weigh 5 pounds or more per pair and are usually referred to as mountaineering boots in catalogues and stores. They are solidly built and almost indestructible, requiring extensive break-in time. It is often joked that hikers do not break in these boots, but the boots break in the hiker's feet instead. You will not wear out a pair of mountaineering boots with normal Trail use, even on a thru-hike, but the extra weight will slow you down considerably and cause leg weariness unless you have very strong legs.

Buying Boots

If you have never before bought hiking boots, you will probably be better off buying them from your local outfitter if you can find a suitable model. Most good outfitters can help you determine your requirements, can fit you properly, and will often allow you to take boots home on trial. When shopping for boots, always try them on with the socks you intend to wear on your hike. If possible, walk around with a loaded pack to see how the boots feel under weighted conditions. Make sure your toes do not jam against the front of the boot when you lunge forward, as you will when going down a mountain. Also make sure that the boot shape fits your arches and verify that the boots bend where your feet bend. Check the heel cup to ensure that its shape matches the curve of your heels, and that it does not bind or rub unduly on the top of either heel. Make sure the uppers do not bind the tendons on the front of your ankles, especially if you have large ankles and lower legs. Rule of thumb: If boots do not feel good in a store, they will not improve on the Trail, so do not buy them. Keep shopping until you find a perfect fit.

Before buying boots, you should ask your dealer about procedures for replacing boots if they should fail (not wear out) on the Trail. If your dealer says that you must return defective boots to the manufacturer for inspection before warranty replacement or repair, look for another brand. Good manufacturers and outfitters will realize that thru-hikers cannot sit around a Trail town for a week or two waiting for new boots, and will agree to replace defective boots promptly, handling any necessary warranty procedures while you are hiking merrily on your way. When your boots eventually wear out, buying new boots from the Trail is not a major problem. You can find an outfitter near the Trail during your hike, or leave buying instructions with your helpers back home before you leave and have them send replacements to you on request. When you purchase your first pair of boots, you may even want to prearrange with your boot dealer to have an identical pair sent later, but allow for the fact that your feet may spread during your hike and a larger and/or wider size may be required for proper fit on up the Trail.

Begin breaking in your boots immediately after you make your purchase, even if the manufacturer claims no break-in time is needed. The secret to breaking in a pair of boots is to put them on and walk and walk and walk and walk. The more you can wear your boots before your hike, the fewer foot problems you will have on the Trail. You also have more opportunity to discover boot defects and improper fit. If you develop blisters during the breaking-in process, a not uncommon occurrence when tender feet meet new boots, remember that these are blisters you will not have on the Trail. During break-in, you can also test to see if insoles offering additional cushioning are needed.

Boot Problems and Care

The mileage estimates for boots given above are just an average based on your author's observations of many hikers over many seasons of thru-hiking. Some hikers are much rougher on boots than others, of course, but even the most light-footed hiker can experience a boot failure. The most common type of boot failure on thru-hikes is separation of the rubber tread from the midsole or upper part of the boot, and all types of boots can suffer this problem, especially during rainy periods when they stay wet day after day. Fortunately, total delamination does not happen all at once but instead happens gradually over a period of days or weeks, usually beginning at the toe or heel of the boot. You can delay the process if you form the habit of inspecting your boots at the end of each hiking day and carry a good boot glue for doing on-the-spot repair as soon as delamination begins. A thru-hiking cobbler recommends "Barge Cement," found in many hardware stores. As for waterproofing your boots, none of the popular products on the market will keep water out of your boots for long, but they will deter it. Small amounts of waterproofing can be carried in a plastic film canister during your hike. Leather boots should be treated often to keep them supple and to prevent cracking as they get wet and dry out repeatedly. Special treatments are available for fabric-leather boots, but few thru-hikers bother to use them.

Choosing Socks

The health of your feet will depend in large part on the socks you choose. Socks for your trip should be designed specifically for backpacking and have padding placed where your feet take the most abuse. Especially important are the areas around the toes, under the ball of the foot, under the boot laces, and around and up the back of the heel. Synthetic-fiber and wool hiking socks are both widely used on the A.T., but cotton socks should be avoided. Most thru-hikers feel that synthetic socks are cooler during hot weather, using them without liners. If you use wool hiking socks, you may want to use a thin, synthetic sock liner (polypropylene in summer, Thermax in winter). Newer wool socks use wool-synthetic blends, which give better performance than pure wool. You should carry as many pairs of socks as you can afford on your thru-hike, or plan to wash a few pairs often. Clean socks have more loft and give better performance, resulting in fewer foot problems and more friends. Brand names of socks frequently seen on the A.T. in recent years are Thor·Lo, Wigwam, and Fox River. *Hint:* If you are using Thor·Lo socks, wash and dry them inside out, and never use chlorine bleach on wool or synthetic socks.

PLANNING STEPS - FOOTWEAR

Step 1. Gather as much information as you can about the boots and socks you must buy before you make any purchases. Visit your local outfitters, and request catalogues from manufacturers and distributors (see page 93 for addresses and telephone numbers).

Step 2. Purchase the socks for your hike, checking on warranty procedures before you make a final purchase.

Step 3. Purchase the boots for your hike, wearing the socks you will wear on your hike while being fitted. Check on warranty procedures before you make a final purchase.

Step 4. Break in your boots, checking for defects and performance of insoles.

Step 5. Pack some leather treatment or boot waterproofing in plastic film canisters or other small containers for use during your hike.

4

Clothing

All too many thru-hikers give little thought to their hiking clothing, assuming that "any old clothes will do in the woods." They fail to realize that the wrong clothes, or not enough clothes, can be very uncomfortable or even dangerous in the mountains. Do not make their mistake. Choose the clothing for your thru-hike carefully, with function instead of fashion in mind, taking into account that on the A.T. it must keep you safe and comfortable in cold, heat, wind, rain, sun, sleet, and snow, and it must give you protection from rocks, limbs, briars, poison ivy, stinging nettles, and insects. In addition, it must be lightweight, durable, quick-drying, and easy to clean.

The specific items of clothing you carry at any given time will depend on the weather, or, to be more precise, the high and low temperatures you expect. Assuming you do a "normal" thru-hike (i.e., starting late March through April from Springer, late May through June from Katahdin), you will probably have some near-freezing days and possibly some nights below freezing. In the middle part of your hike, you will have summer conditions. At the conclusion of your hike, you will probably have cold temperatures again, depending on when you finish. Northbounders should keep in mind that freak winter-like storms can occur in the Southern mountains at any time in early spring. Flowers may be blooming one day and snow falling the next. Those starting in late February or early March should be prepared for extreme weather, possibly one or more feet of snow and near-zero temperatures at the higher elevations, especially in the Smokies. In recent years, heavy snowfalls have occurred in the South between mid-March and early April, with one storm in early May. Southbounders should call Baxter State Park for an up-to-date reading of recent Maine weather, which is virtually unpredictable from year to year. For statistical information about temperatures and precipitation along the Trail, see the "Climate and Weather Chart" on page 87, remembering that the figures shown are averages. Actual temperatures at any given time can fall substantially below those shown. Rule of thumb: Always plan your clothing for the worst weather conditions you can expect and allow for a few surprises as well.

Clothing Requirements

Your clothing will involve both warm-weather and cold-weather clothes in various combinations as you move through the seasons. You will also need rainwear, and you may want to include special clothes for wear in Trail towns as well. Your selection of individual clothing items should be guided by the concept of layering, meaning the use of several thinner layers of clothing together to create thicker layers. Layering gives you the ability to adjust insulation and ventilation as your body heat increases or decreases with activity. This is very important on a thru-hike. For example, when climbing a mountain and generating a lot of heat and perspiration, you can strip down to a single layer. When sitting around camp and producing less body heat, or when hiking in cool and/or windy conditions, you can add layers for warmth. In very cold weather, you can add many layers to keep warm. Layering allows you to use a few well-chosen garments to keep comfortable in any weather at any level of activity. Most thru-hikers use a three-layer system as follows:
• *Inner wicking layer:* underwear or lightweight garments of a material that provides some insulation and has good wicking qualities to keep perspiration moisture away from your skin.
• *Middle insulating layer:* heavier garments, such as sweaters or pile jackets and pants, or lightweight down garments, to keep you warm without trapping body moisture.
• *Outer protective layer:* waterproof-windproof parkas and pants, often unlined and without insulation, to protect the inner and/or middle layers from the elements, usually constructed of a breathable material.

Warm-weather Clothing
Most of your trip will be hiked in sunny, warm weather with no rain (really, it will!). On such days, you will wear a shirt, shorts, socks, boots, and little else. The shirt and shorts you use should be lightweight and easily washed,

made of quick-dry nylon or similar material, and they should be loose to allow freedom of movement. You should have at least two sets, perhaps more in hot weather. A long-sleeved shirt will feel good in camp and deter insects. Underpants are optional and unneeded for hiking if your shorts have a built-in brief. Cotton underpants should be avoided for hiking, but make a comfortable set of Trail pajamas and help keep your sleeping bag clean. Many women hikers use a hiking or jogging bra, but many do not. You may want to have a pair of lightweight long pants to protect against sunburn early in the trip, and they are useful for protection from insects and stinging nettles later. A lightweight jacket (windbreaker-type or equivalent) is needed to prevent chilling when you stop for breaks, except in the hottest weather, and a lightweight wool sweater or equivalent garment feels good in camp on many evenings. During the hottest summer months, either the jacket or sweater can be sent home, but plan to have one of them with you at all times. Many thru-hikers include a cap, and find that crushable soft-brim types works best.

Cold-weather Clothing

The time of year you start and end your hike, and the direction you choose for doing your hike, will determine how much cold-weather clothing you need. If you plan a normal start, remember that you will have mostly cool-to-warm days, but days and evenings can drop below freezing occasionally, and you may have some snow and extended cold at the higher elevations. In addition to the warm-weather clothing items above, you will need to add lightweight or medium-weight thermal underwear (synthetic, not cotton). You may want to substitute a heavier sweater or equivalent garment for the lightweight sweater, and you may want to carry an insulated parka instead of the lightweight jacket. A ski cap is a necessity (the first cold-weather item you should put on while hiking), and gloves feel good in cold, windy conditions. This combination of warm- and cold-weather clothing should be sufficient for any early-spring weather conditions you will encounter in the South. In the rare event you get caught in more severe weather, you can always lay over in a shelter and stay in your sleeping bag until conditions improve, or head for the nearest town. Southbounders may have to use slightly warmer clothing if Maine is having a cold spring. If you plan to start your hike earlier than the normal period mentioned above, you will need to get information about doing a winter hike, which is beyond the scope of this discussion. Keep in mind that winter conditions above 3,000 feet can be brutal even in the southern Appalachians. Do not risk your life if you have never had experience living outdoors for extended periods in below-zero conditions; wait for warmer weather.

Rainwear

You will need some type of rainwear for an A.T. thru-hike, not so much for keeping dry as for keeping warm on cool, windy, rainy days. Most thru-hikers use a rain jacket and pants, constructed from either a breathable or coated-nylon fabric. They can then wear jacket, pants, or both as conditions require. A rain jacket with zippered underarms is very helpful in controlling body heat and perspiration. A few people use chaps instead of rain pants to save weight, but chaps have the disadvantage of having to be tied to a belt or something else to hold them up. Some thru-hiker's use a poncho, which is not ideal rain protection in windy conditions and cannot be easily adjusted to protect against windchill effects, but it is a satisfactory and inexpensive alternative to the higher-priced rain suits. Gaiters will help keep water out of your boots, but are normally used by thru-hikers only in cooler weather. Whichever type of rainwear you select, know that nothing will keep you dry from your own sweat when you are hiking up a steep mountain with a pack. In hot weather, you will probably choose to leave your rainwear in your pack when it rains.

Town Clothes

Some thru-hikers carry a set of town clothes in addition to their Trail clothing. This is purely optional, depending somewhat on your dedication to fashion. Town clothes can be simply a spare set of shorts and shirt that you use only for town wear, or you may want to include some lightweight "dress" clothes. Many thru-hikers like the feel of something other than hiking attire in towns, especially when they go out to dine or catch a movie. Even if they do not want to carry special town clothes, most thru-hikers do find a pair of sandals or sneakers worth the added weight. Sandals or sneakers are a welcome change from wet boots in town and feel equally good in camp. If you choose sandals, pick the open-toe kind you can wear with socks in cooler temperatures. Brands of sandals popular with thru-hikers are Teva and Birkenstock. A few recent hikers have used aquasocks for camp and town wear, but select the breatheable kind if you use them.

Choosing Clothing

The first step in choosing the clothing to use on your thru-hike is to make a clothing list of every item you think you will need for your hike. A sample clothing checklist is illustrated on pages 62-63 to assist you. It lists the essential items needed to begin an A.T. thru-hike, based on a survey of what many past thru-hikers have retained in their packs a few weeks after they have begun their hikes and had time to send unnecessary items home. Notice that the sample clothing checklist has space for recording the weight of each item, to help monitor total clothing weight, and you should do so as you select your clothes. Once you have a list of clothing for your hike that satisfies you, compare the listed items with the clothing items you have on hand. This will tell you which items you need to research and buy. Be careful about adding items to your clothing list, even more so than you were when making your equipment list. A few items of unnecessary or inappropriate clothing (for example, that favorite pair of jeans) can add several pounds to your pack weight, quickly offsetting any advantage gained by selecting lightweight equipment. As you did with your equipment list, you should revise and refine your clothing list until you arrive at a combination "on paper" that meets your hiking requirements, and minimizes the weight added to your overall pack weight, before you make any purchases.

Resist the temptation to rush out and buy a completely new backpacking wardrobe. There may be many clothing items already in your closet that are quite suitable for use on your hike, especially if you are active in other outdoor activities. Soccer uniforms, for instance, make excellent hiking clothing. On the other hand, many sportswear items are made of cotton, which is generally unsuitable for use on the Trail because it absorbs perspiration and takes forever to dry, undesirable properties in cool or cold weather. Undoubtedly you will want to consider clothing, made especially for backpacking, which incorporates designs and materials created to handle the special needs of hikers. You can best obtain information about the latest available backpacking clothing by visiting outfitters in your area and looking at clothing items in person. Some of the materials used for making backpacking clothing that have proven popular among thru-hikers in recent years are:
- *Gore-Tex fabric:* a breathable membrane, laminated to nylon cloth, which keeps out wind and water droplets but allows water vapor from perspiration to pass through; used in a variety of clothing items, especially rainwear.
- *Ultrex fabric:* a waterproof, windproof, breathable fabric system; used in a variety of clothing items, especially rainwear.
- *Urethane/PVC cloth:* plastic-coated nylon cloth that is waterproof and windproof but not breathable; used in a variety of clothing items, especially inexpensive rainwear.
- *Polypropylene:* a synthetic fiber that will not absorb water, touted for its wicking properties; used in a variety of clothing items, especially underwear and liner socks. *Capilene* is a variation used by Patagonia.
- *PolarTec:* a resilient fleece-like fabric, available in varying thicknesses, with excellent breathability and insulating qualities; used primarily in jackets, pants, gloves, and caps. *Synchilla* is a variation used by Patagonia.
- *Supplex:* a nylon cloth that has the soft feel of cotton; used especially in shirts and hiking shorts.
- *Thermax:* a hollow-core fiber that transfers perspiration through the fabric while providing thermal insulation for warmth; used especially in underwear and liner socks.
- *Thinsulate:* a material made of ultra-fine fibers with lots of air pockets, providing excellent insulation without bulk; used primarily in outerwear and gloves.

Buying Clothing

You will have two main sources for buying backpacking clothing: mail-order catalogues and your local outfitters. Mail-order catalogues sometimes offer more variety but may not save you much money, especially after you pay shipping charges, since many brand-name clothing items seem to be priced about the same no matter where you buy them. Your local outfitter will normally have fewer choices of clothing, but you will be able to try on items and make sure they fit. You will probably be better off buying major clothing items (rainwear, parka, *etc.*) from a local outfitter if you have never had experience with these items.

Back-up Clothing

As the weather changes from spring to summer and then to autumn, you may need to add to, subtract from, or change the clothing items you are carrying. Back-up clothing should be packaged, numbered, and listed as you did back-up equipment, so that it can be sent without error when you request it from home. Most northbounders send cold-weather gear home from somewhere in southern Virginia, and pick up cold-weather gear for going through the White Mountains at Hanover or Glencliff, New Hampshire. Southbounders usually send cold-weather gear home from Hanover, after they have gone through the Whites, and pick it back up somewhere in southern Virginia prior to going through the southern Appalachian highlands and the Smokies.

Clothes Bag

A stuff sack is needed as a clothes bag for keeping your clean clothing together in your pack, and it makes an excellent pillow at no additional weight. Your clothes bag should be carried in a plastic bag, so that you will always have at least one set of dry clothes protected in plastic in case of emergency. Dirty clothing, which is often wet and sweaty, should be stored in a separate plastic bag.

PLANNING STEPS - CLOTHING

Step 1. Make a list of every piece of clothing you think you will need for doing your thru-hike, using the sample clothing checklist shown on pages 62-63 as a guide.

Step 2. Inventory the clothing items you already have on hand and want to use on your hike, rejecting the items made of cotton.

Step 3. Compare the two lists to reveal which items you must buy before you start your hike.

Step 4. Gather as much information as you can about the items you must buy before you make any purchases. Visit you local outfitters to check out their clothing lines.

Step 5. Work with your clothing list "on paper" until you have the ideal clothing combination for starting and continuing your hike.

Step 6. Purchase the clothing for your trip, checking on warranty procedures before you make final purchases.

Step 7. Make a list of back-up clothing, numbering and listing items as described in the discussion section.

Step 8. Purchase or make a stuff sack to use as a clothes bag for all of your clothing items. You may want to have a smaller stuff sack to hold your socks if you are carrying many pairs.

Step 9. Write your name in permanent ink on your major clothing items, or sew in custom name-labels.

Step 10. Check washing instructions for your major garments, and record special instructions in your *Data Book* or *Handbook* for reference on the Trail.

5

Food and Supplies

The typical thru-hiker eats 250-400 pounds of food and uses thirty pounds of supplies during an end-to-end hike. You may need even more. Since you obviously cannot carry that much weight with you from the start of your hike, you will have to obtain food and supplies as you go along. If you have read accounts of thru-hikes done in the 1950s or 1960s, you may recall that many of those pioneer thru-hikers used a system of caches buried at road crossings as their primary means of resupplying. This method worked well then, when there were not many facilities near the Trail, but such caches are unnecessary on today's Trail and are discouraged for environmental reasons. The latter is also true of "living off the land," which is something that is almost impossible for thru-hikers to do since daily long-distance hiking leaves no time to forage and hunt. Several years ago, for example, one young man left Springer Mountain with no food, intending to live by snaring small animals and foraging for plants, almost starving for five days before he reached a telephone to "snare" his parent's Visa card!

Resupplying

There are several easy ways to obtain food and supplies on a thru-hike, and all involve using grocery stores or post offices along the Trail, either exclusively or in combination. Your choice of which method to use will be determined by the kind of food you want to eat and the way you want to do your hike. One of the following resupply methods will best suit the way your requirements:

Grocery stores: The simplest way of resupplying during your hike is to purchase everything you need from grocery stores and supermarkets near the Trail. Using this method, you will not have to plan meal menus before your hike since meals are dictated *en route* by availability of items in stores, and you can easily vary your diet to suit changing food preferences over the course of your journey. You will have to be adaptable, though, since the items you prefer may not always be available in small stores or may not be available in the small quantities you need. Prices will often be considerably higher than you pay back home unless you live in a major metropolitan area, in which case prices may actually be lower. On the other hand, you will not have to pay postage for mailing food packages or make arrangements for having them mailed.

Maildrops: The surest way of resupplying is to have food packages mailed to yourself from home and pick them up at post offices in towns near the Trail. Using this method, you are assured of having exactly the items you need in the quantities you need. Specialty items, which are often impossible to find in many Trail communities, are as easy to include as regular fare. The nutritional value of your meals can be better controlled using maildrops, but you will have to plan menus before you begin your hike, of course, and you will have to estimate the quantities of food you will need once you develop a Trail appetite. You can also include small quantities of supplies in your food packages. The cost of postage for mailing packages can be offset somewhat by buying food and supplies in bulk.

Combination method: The most popular method of resupplying is to use a combination of maildrops and grocery-store purchases. This combination method allows great flexibility. For example, you can mail nutritious breakfast and supper items in your maildrop packages and buy easy-to-find lunch and snack items from grocery stores to provide variety. A variation used by many thru-hikers is to use maildrops at smaller locations with limited facilities and buy from grocery stores and supermarkets at locations where suitable facilities are available.

33

Choosing Food

The food you eat on your hike is the fuel that will keep you going, both physically and mentally, so it should be planned as carefully as you plan equipment, footwear, and clothing. Your choice of food will be determined by a combination of factors: nutrition, ease of preparation, cooking time (fuel consumption), weight, taste appeal, and cost. The individual items of food seen in the food bags of thru-hikers are as diverse as the hikers themselves, but several types of food are seen often:

- *Processed food:* This type of food is found on the shelves of grocery stores and supermarkets, primarily in the form of dinners, side dishes, mixes, canned meats, cereals, and dry staples (pasta, rice, *etc.*) that need no refrigeration. It is slightly heavier than freeze-dried food in weight per meal, requires more cooking, but costs considerably less. Most thru-hikers use processed foods for the majority of their meals, whether they buy them before or during their hikes.
- *Freeze-dried food:* This type of food is usually found at backpacking or survivalist stores. It was developed for the space program back in the 1960s, and is normally produced by vacuum drying frozen precooked meals. The resultant meals are very lightweight (they contain virtually no water) and need only hot water for reconstitution, but they are expensive per meal, and reconstitution is not always perfect, especially where meats are concerned.
- *Specialty food:* This type of food is available from food outlets specializing in backpacking foods (usually mail-order), and most offer a wide variety of menu items designed to be cooked with backpacking stoves and cooksets. Many thru-hikers who use prepackaged Trail foods prefer these specialty foods to freeze-dried foods. Some suppliers sell in bulk and will arrange to ship food to you on the Trail.
- *Natural food:* This type of food is found in natural- or organic-food stores, and, since it has no additives or chemical preservatives, is sometimes referred to as "health food." Often these food outlets have a variety of unusual mixes and products suitable for backpacking not available in regular grocery stores or supermarkets, and most offer a good selection of commercially dried and dehydrated products.
- *Self-dehydrated food:* This type of food is the most personalized since it is usually produced by the user at home. A few thru-hikers each year dehydrate all of the food they use on the Trail, and this method of preparation seems to work quite well, depending on the experience of the preparer. Many natural-food stores have books on preparing dehydrated food.
- *Fresh food:* This type of food can be purchased in Trail towns during your hike and carried on the Trail for several days without refrigeration, especially fruits, vegetables, cheeses, and margarine.

Meal Menus

If you plan to use maildrops for resupplying, either partially or totally, you will need to plan menus for the Trail meals you will eat on your hike. A sample menu planner is illustrated on page 64 to assist you. You should plan at least nine different meal menus, three each for breakfast, lunch, and supper. Some thru-hikers plan more, to give them variety on the Trail. Most, like your author, use a few basic menus and eat essentially the same thing every day, with minor variations in flavor and components (a good supply of spices comes in handy, if you know how to use them). The important thing is to keep your menus simple in order to conserve both cooking time and fuel consumption. Later in your planning, after you have drafted your hiking schedule, you will use the menus on your menu planner to calculate the individual food items you will need to buy for your hike.

Breakfast: A nutritious breakfast is as much a necessity on the Trail as at home, but simplicity is equally important if you do not want to spend all morning cooking in camp instead of hiking. Many thru-hikers limit breakfast cooking to boiling water to add to prepackaged cereals, though a few do enjoy eating more elaborate cooked meals every morning. In warm weather, most thru-hikers eat a cold breakfast, which has just as much nutrition and energy. You should choose breakfast items that can be eaten either hot or cold during the summer months. Frequently used breakfast components include granola cereals and bars, regular cereals, instant-breakfast mixes, instant oatmeal, instant grits, cream of wheat, pancakes, French toast, Pop-Tarts, powdered milk, honey, margarine (added to cereals or pancakes to taste), bagels and cream cheese, instant coffee, hot cocoa, and Postum.

Lunch: A good lunch around midday and/or several smaller snacks during the day will be required to keep your energy level up. Few thru-hikers cook lunch unless the weather is cold. In that case, they heat water for soup and beverages. Once the weather warms, virtually no one eats a hot lunch on the Trail. Frequently used lunch components include loaf bread, pita bread, English muffins, bagels, hard cheeses, cream cheese, crackers of all types, peanut butter, jelly, sardines, canned meats, Vienna sausages, deli-type sausages, beef jerky, instant soups, cookies, snack foods of all types, dried fruit, Trail mixes (usually "gorp" made from peanuts, raisins, and M&Ms), powdered drink mixes, and hot Jello as a beverage on cool days.

Supper: A hot supper is preferred by most thru-hikers, as much for morale as for nourishment. In fact, the only thing that will keep you going on some of the rougher afternoons is the thought of a tasty supper at the end of your ordeal. Suppers should be easy to prepare, preferably needing only one pot for preparation, since often you will have to cook your evening meal when you are very tired and/or the shelter is crowded. Many thru-hikers eat several courses (soup, glop, and dessert), cooking one item and eating it before cooking another. If you are typical, you will eat your supper early, around 5 p.m., then nibble on snacks for the rest of the evening. Thru-hikers occasionally share components to cook group suppers at shelters. These occasions are socially rewarding, and the culinary results are often tasty. Frequently used supper components include mac-and-cheese dinners, Lipton Pasta and Sauce dinners, Lipton Rice and Sauce dinners, Minute Rice or instant potatoes with soup or gravy mixes, Ramen noodles, Stove-top Stuffing, canned tuna/chicken/ham, dried beef, Vienna sausages, deli-type sausages, beef jerky, hard cheeses, Jello chilled in spring or stream, instant pudding and cheesecake, dried fruit, cookies, gorp, powdered milk, and squeeze margarine or butter. Some thru-hikers use the military ready-to-eat meals, but often find they are fairly heavy for the calories provided, and the quantities may be small for a hungry thru-hiker.

Calories and Nutrition

How many calories will you need per day? Some thru-hikers eat like birds and seem to have plenty of energy. Others eat as many as 7,000+ calories a day and still want more. The average seems to be about 3,000 to 3,500 calories a day, and that will be a good range to use for your planning. You can use the "Trail Food Calorie Chart" on page 88 to estimate the calorie content of each meal as you plan your menus, assuming you choose to eat common trail foods. If it turns out that you require more calories than planned, you can always buy more high-calorie items along the way to supplement your basic menus. And, believe me, you will be concerned with eating enough calories for most of your trip, being able to eat anything in almost any amount without fear of gaining weight. Nutrition is also very important on an extended hike. Although there are no statistics to prove it, observation indicates that most thru-hikers who "run out of steam," either physically or mentally, do so mainly as a result of poor nutritional habits. You should try to maintain the following ratio in your basic diet: 10% protein, 60% carbohydrate, and 30% fat. The protein and carbohydrate requirements are easy to meet with standard trail foods, but you may have to carry squeeze margarine or oils to provide much of the necessary fat, especially later in your hike when your lean body craves fatty foods. A one-a-day-type multivitamin and mineral supplement is good insurance that you are getting the essential vitamins and minerals you need, though megadoses are not required. Many women thru-hikers claim that calcium supplements are beneficial. Town visits will afford opportunities for eating things you cannot eat regularly on the Trail, such as fresh vegetables and fruits.

Calculating Food Quantities

The total food quantities needed for your hike can be calculated after you have identified the meal source for each meal you will eat during your hike. The latter can be done by using your scheduling forms, once you have finalized your prehike schedule. The scheduling forms have columns marked B, L, and S (see pages 67-72). These are the abbreviations for breakfast, lunch, and supper, and you will need to eat one of each meal for each day of your trip. The food for these meals must come from somewhere, either maildrops, grocery stores, or restaurants, or they must be included with your overnight lodging. You can identify the source for each meal by placing a meal-source symbol (x=meal from maildrop, G=meal from grocery store, R=meal from restaurant,

A=meal included with lodging) in the space provided on the scheduling form. For simplicity, list opposite a destination the meals you will eat during the day following an overnight stay at that destination, beginning with the breakfast you eat that morning and ending with the supper you will eat at the next overnight destination. When you have determined the source for each individual meal, you can then determine the total maildrop meals required for your trip and the total meals required for placement in each maildrop. Keep in mind that these calculations are only estimates. They will be close, but you may still have to buy extra food items from time to time on the Trail because your schedule and appetite will vary somewhat from your plans.

Total food: After you have identified the needed number of meals from maildrops, you can calculate the total quantities of each food item you must buy for your hike from the meal columns on your scheduling forms. This is a simple process of counting the total number of maildrop breakfasts, lunches, and suppers your schedule indicates you will need (snacks can be estimated), assigning how many of each meal listed on your menu planner you want to use, and then listing the components. A food list is illustrated on page 65 to assist you. Once the components are listed, multiply by the number of meals needed to find the bulk quantities needed. For example, if you need 168 breakfasts from maildrops during your hike and want to use breakfast menu #1 (Pop-Tarts and coffee) for 68 of those breakfasts, then list each component and multiply by 68, showing that you need 68 Pop-Tarts and 68 servings of coffee. An alternate method is to use your maildrop packing lists, calculating the quantities for each maildrop and transferring the total of all components packed in maildrops to your food list (see section below).

Maildrop packing lists: The quantities of meal components and other foods to be included in each maildrop can be listed once you have determined meal sources for each meal and picked your maildrop locations. This is a simple procedure. For example, to list the breakfasts needed in each maildrop, prepare a maildrop packing list for breakfast (see sample illustrated on page 73). You will need to list your maildrop locations on this list. Using your prehike scheduling form, count the "x's" in the "B" column between one maildrop location and the next. The total number of "x's" is the number of breakfasts that you should pack in the maildrop being sent to the first of the two locations. Record that number of breakfasts next to the maildrop location and list the components needed to furnish that number of breakfasts. The total number of breakfasts and components listed on your maildrop packing list should match the total-needed number of breakfasts and components listed on your food list. Lunches, suppers, and other foods in each maildrop can be listed in the same manner.

Emergency food: An extra meal or day's supply of food should be carried with you at all times. This is especially important in cooler weather. In very cold weather, or in the most remote areas along the Trail, you may want to carry a two-day's supply of extra food. Emergency food does not have to be packed in your maildrops since you can easily buy extra items in towns as you go along, depending on the need. Most thru-hikers carry one extra dinner and some gorp as their emergency food supply. One clever, but eccentric, individual carried a small bag of dried dog food as his emergency ration. Why? It had the necessary calories for survival and he knew he would never be tempted to eat it unless he had a real emergency!

Buying Food

You can usually save money by buying food in bulk before your hike. Catalogue outfitters, and some local outfitters, sell bulk quantities of freeze-dried and dehydrated foods that you can repackage. If you are using mostly processed foods, many large towns have a discount-food warehouse or co-op. The savings when buying in bulk can be substantial compared to buying in smaller stores along the Trail. In general, you will find smaller stores in some Trail towns in the South, especially below middle Virginia, and in Maine. Just about everywhere else, you will be able to reach a large supermarket without too much trouble. The *Handbook* lists all stores near the A.T. and gives information about their suitability for resupplying. Vegetarians can find acceptable items in most large towns but should not count on finding an abundance of suitable items in smaller stores, especially in the southern Appalachians. After you have been on the Trail for a few weeks, going into grocery stores of any size will be one of the real delights of your trip.

Food and Supplies

Protecting Food

You should plan to carry your food in a nylon bag, since you will often have to hang it for protection from animals. When camping away from a shelter in bear country, you will need to hang your food bag from a tree—at least 15 feet above the ground and five feet away from both the trunk and the supporting limb—or, better yet, loop a cord over limbs on two trees and suspend your bag between the trees. In shelters, your food bag will need to be protected from mice and skunks. Hanging it by a cord from a rafter nail is usually sufficient, but sometimes more elaborate measures are required. A plastic-bag liner inside your food bag will give protection from the elements when you hang it outside your tent on a stormy night.

Choosing Supplies

You can save money and pack weight by including supplies in your maildrop packages, thus preventing you from having to buy a giant-sized whatever (for example, toothpaste) in Trail towns and carry the extra weight in your pack or throw away the excess before leaving town. The supplies and miscellaneous items needed by thru-hikers vary as much as food items, but everyone needs a few basic items. A roll of toilet paper should be placed in every maildrop package, along with plastic garbage bags for protecting your sleeping bag and clothing, a large Ziploc-type bag for your garbage, small Ziploc-type bags for repackaging food, as well as film, notebooks to continue your journal, and any other items you regularly use but need only in small quantities. Be careful with soaps or detergents (or scented toilet paper) packed in maildrops. Perfumed types can taint food items, making everything taste like soap. Use only unscented detergent and toilet paper. Note that many WalMart, K-Mart, drugstores, and many supermarkets have a special section of travel-sized toiletry items that are ideal for backpacking.

Supplies and miscellaneous items can be most easily calculated by listing them on your maildrop packing lists in the same manner as for food items above (see samples illustrated on pages 77-78). Using your hiking schedule to calculate the days between maildrops, you can then estimate the quantity of each item needed at each maildrop location. Simply figure how many days from one maildrop to the next and calculate the quantity needed based on your expected use of each item per day. Enter the required quantity next to the appropriate location on the list. You may not need to include every listed supply item in every maildrop if the quantities used per day are small. The total quantities of supplies and miscellaneous items listed on your maildrop packing lists can be listed on your supplies and miscellaneous items list to calculate the total cost of these items for your hike (see sample illustrated on page 66).

PLANNING STEPS - FOOD AND SUPPLIES

Step 1. Decide on the method of resupplying you will use on your hike. If you decide to use maildrops, either partially or totally, proceed with the steps outlined below.

Step 2. Plan menus for use on your hike, using the sample menu planner on page 64 as a guide. As you are planning your menus, calculate the calories for each meal, using the "Trail Food Calorie Chart" on page 88 to assist you.

Step 3. Calculate the total number of breakfasts, lunches, and suppers from your hiking schedule once you have finalized your schedule and picked your maildrops. Decide how many of each meal listed on your menu planner you will use. For example, if you have four breakfast menus, you may want to use three of them often and one only occasionally.

(planning steps continued on next page)

Step 4. Itemize on your food list the menu components of each meal listed on your menu planner, using the sample food list on page 65 as a guide, and list the number of meals in which each component is used. Some components will be used for more than one meal, but should be listed only once on the food list, changing the number-needed figure to account for the component's multiple-meal use.

Step 5. List food components on the appropriate maildrop packing lists, using the sample maildrop packing lists shown on pages 73-76 as guides, double-checking to make sure the quantities agree with the quantities on your food list.

Step 6. Multiply the number-needed figure for each meal component by the quantity per meal for the component, arriving at the total quantity you need to purchase for packing in your maildrops.

Step 7. Shop around to find the best prices for each component, then calculate the total price for each component. The sum of these total component prices will give you the total cost of food for packing in your maildrops.

Step 8. List the supplies and miscellaneous items you plan to use on your hike. A supplies and miscellaneous items list is illustrated on page 66 to assist you. The maildrop packing lists for supplies and miscellaneous items (illustrated on pages 77-78) are useful in determining the total quantities, by calculating the sum of the quantities you will pack in each maildrop.

Step 9. Shop around to find the best unit price for supplies and miscellaneous items, and then use that figure to calculate the total cost of these items for packing in your maildrops.

Step 10. Buy the food, supplies, and miscellaneous items for packing in your maildrops, preferably a minimum of several weeks before your plan to start your hike.

Step 11. Package bulk components into the smaller units you will use in each maildrop, using your maildrop packing lists as a guide. For example, if you are using powdered milk each day, you may choose to package a big bag with a "one-maildrop" supply, or you may choose to package the exact quantity you will use each day in smaller "daily" packages. Some thru-hikers find it useful to package each day's meal components together in a large Ziploc-type bag.

Step 12. Count the packages of food and supplies to verify that you have enough of each to pack in your maildrops.

6

Health and Hygiene

The thru-hiker who has no minor sickness or injury on a six-month journey is the exception. Most have a head cold or sore throat, or a bruise or cut, along the way. Even major illness and injury are possibilities, since going into the woods for months on end has inherent risks. Predicting if and when the more serious events may happen to you on a thru-hike is impossible, so worrying about them accomplishes nothing. Your energies will best be spent preparing for good health and hygiene on your trip.

Health Guidelines

A medical checkup is always a good idea before attempting a thru-hike. Common sense makes it mandatory for the older hiker. If you know beforehand that you have a special medical problem, such as diabetes, you should discuss treatment on a thru-hike with your doctor. A dental checkup is also a good idea, and dental problems should be corrected. It is much easier to have dental work done at home rather than on the Trail. You should begin preparing your body for the long haul as soon as you have medical clearance to do your hike, though Olympic-type preparations are not necessary, and any conditioning you can do at home before your hike will benefit you on the Trail. You should select an exercise program that does at least two things at the minimum. First, it should build up your lung capacity by working the large muscle groups, especially the legs. Second, and most important, it should toughen your tender feet (the source of most physical problems in the early going). Short of going up and down mountains with a pack, which is the only way to totally prepare for doing a thru-hike, the best single exercise is vigorous walking with boots, with or without a pack, on natural terrain. As with all exercise, begin slowly and use moderation, and plan to do the same at the beginning of your thru-hike.

Common Ailments

There are a number of ailments that seem to be common among beginning thru-hikers. Almost everyone has blisters sooner or later, of course, and many have chafing under pack straps and belt, and between the legs. Quite a few have a head cold during the first week or two of their hike. Sunburn is not uncommon, since trees are still leafless on mountain ridges early in the year, and sunburn is usually accompanied by chapped lips. Acid stomach plagues a number of hikers early in their hike as they are adjusting to Trail food. Later in the season, many hikers have a minor case of poison ivy. Pollen allergies are frequent in spring and autumn, even among hikers who are not normally bothered. Diarrhea strikes a few hikers, probably due to the accumulated stress of the trip more than anything else. Few, if any, cases of *giardia* or hypothermia are seen from year to year, and snakebite and Lyme disease are extremely rare, statistically almost nonexistent.

Many of the minor physical ailments that are seen often among thru-hikers each year involve the feet, knees, legs, and hips, since these parts of the body take such a beating on a long hike. Blackened toenails are quite common, caused by the toes jamming into the front end of boots, and a fair number of thru-hikers temporarily lose a toenail or two. Numbness in the various areas of the feet, especially the toes and ball of the foot, is quite common, caused by the repeated pounding from as many as 30,000 steps a day. Numbness of the hips and upper thighs is another problem frequently mentioned, caused by pack belt pressure. And, as you would expect, sore knees are experienced by everyone sooner or later. Although annoying, none of these ailments are usually permanent, but you should stop hiking and seek medical attention if the pain becomes severe. A more serious problem, in that it can end your hike, is a case of shin splints (severe pain on the front of the leg just above the top of your boot), which almost always occurs in the first few hundred miles of a thru-hike and is more prevalent in wet, muddy years. Rest is the only real cure, and medical attention is advised. The same can be said for an inflamed Achilles tendon, a problem that bothers a handful of thru-hikers each year. Though you may be able to continue hiking at a reduced pace, albeit with considerable pain, doing so with shin splints or an inflamed Achilles tendon can result in permanent damage that may limit your participation in future activities. Do not take that risk; listen to your body and doctor.

If you do experience a disabling illness or injury on the A.T., you will never be far from help in terms of both hours and miles. The fear of breaking an ankle or leg and laying injured and alone for days in the woods is often felt but never experienced, especially during the thru-hiker season. There are just too many other people using the Trail for you to remain isolated for long. Sending for help is usually a simple matter of having someone walk to the nearest road crossing or homestead. Most neighboring communities have rescue services that can handle any situation. In Trail towns, just ask townspeople for their nearest doctor, dentist, or emergency room.

First-aid Kit

Some thru-hikers carry huge first-aid kits, capable of handling almost any medical emergency. In theory, this is fine, but in practice they use very little of the more serious medicines and bandages and end up discarding everything but the essentials as they go along. Your first-aid kit should be able to handle any of the common ailments mentioned in the section above, and it should be able to handle minor injury. A first-aid kit checklist is provided on page 61 to assist you in selecting items for your kit. It lists the basic items needed to treat most minor A.T. problems. If you do have a large wound or major injury on your trip, you will need additional bandages, but these can be improvised. For instance, you can tear up some of your clothing or equipment to make large bandages and slings. You can also use moleskin and Second Skin, or even toilet paper, wrapped with your Ace bandage, to cover large wounds until you get medical attention. In other words, you can plan to be adaptable and save pack weight. If you have special medical problems, you should add any items or medicines needed to take care of those problems, no matter the weight. Those with thyroid disorders should probably stay away from iodine water-purification products, or, at the least, get medical approval.

Health Hazards

You may experience one or more of the following hazards to your health on your hike. If you experience more than a few, you may be jinxed! The following section of on-Trail instructions is included in the *Handbook*, so you will have it available for reference during your hike. It is included here so that you can take note of items you may want to consider for inclusion in your first-aid kit.

Blisters are preventable, so be alert for "hot spots." Apply moleskin at the first indication of tenderness, then tighten boots to prevent slippage. If a blister should develop, first wash the area, then apply antibiotic ointment. Sterilize a needle in a flame, and drain the swollen area from the edge. Try not to tear the distended skin. Apply more antibiotic ointment, cover with a sterile pad (or Second Skin by Spenco), then cover the pad with a larger piece of moleskin. If the distended skin is badly torn, treat as above but trim the torn skin before covering. In either case, change the dressing at least daily, to prevent infection.

Chafing is a very painful condition most often caused by the pressure of pack straps and waist belts against the skin or by skin rubbing against skin between the legs. It is usually aggravated by sweat. The best treatment for mild cases is the application of corn starch or medicated powder. If you are sweating profusely, a Vaseline-type ointment may be more effective. At the end of the day, wash the chafed area, apply a light coating of antibiotic cream, and expose to air. Also, during the hottest months, you may want to carry a small tube of skin cream to alleviate rectal inflammation, a very painful condition encountered by many thru-hikers each year, making them "walk like a cowboy" until they can get relief.

Athlete's foot can be neglected for a few hours back home, but, if left untreated even briefly while thru-hiking, it can cause major problems. Stop immediately, and wash the infected area before applying a fungicide. If possible, change to clean socks. Apply more medicine, and air your feet every time you take a rest break. Jock itch is another form of the same infection and is treated in a similar manner.

Poison ivy is an easily recognized plant ("leaves of three, let them be") abundant along the Trail. Any time you come into contact with the sap by bruising or brushing a plant in any season, you can have an allergic reaction. Symptoms are an itch and reddening skin, followed by seeping blisters. The problem can last for several days. When first exposed, wash the area with a non-oily soap. Treat with an over-the-counter lotion designed specifically for poison ivy. If these measures do not work in a few days, you should seek medical help, before the problem gets out of hand.

Ticks are bloodsuckers that usually get on you in high-grass areas. They do not attach immediately, so chances are you will be able to simply pick them off. If one does attach, however, you must gently extract the critter. Use care not to mash the tick's body fluids back into your bloodstream or break off its head under your skin. Try holding the glowing end of an extinguished match next to the tick, or try to suffocate it by covering its body with oil or insect repellent. If one of these measures does not make the tick release, you will need to use tweezers. After removal, wash and treat the bite as you would any puncture wound.

Lyme disease is caused by a bacterium transmitted by the painless bite of the deer tick, which is about the size of the letter "o" on this page. The tick must stay attached from 10 to 12 hours (some claim as much as 36 hours) to pass on this still-rare infection. Shortly after infection, many folks seem to have flu-like symptoms such as headache, stiff neck, fever, muscle aches, fatigue, and vomiting. Sometimes a rash will appear days or even weeks later-often raised, red, and doughnut-shaped around the bite-or it can appear in various shapes anywhere on the body. Later symptoms include stiff joints and swollen glands. Your doctor may not immediately think to look for Lyme disease, so mention the possibility of exposure when you seek treatment for these or similar symptoms.

Insect bites are rarely a problem on the A.T., either while hiking or in camp, much to the surprise of many thru-hikers. Mosquitoes and no-see-ums can be bothersome in midsummer on an occasional evening, and, from time to time, a persistent deer fly or swarm of gnats can seem to follow you for miles as you hike, but these are the main irritants you will encounter in normal years. Few thru-hikers report trouble from chiggers, spiders, ants, and other non-stinging insects. The exception is the northern blackfly, which can inflict a serious bite. Southbounders going through New England in spring and early summer should take measures to protect themselves, usually with a good repellant and clothing. Northbounders normally arrive in blackfly country after the swarming season.

Stings from insects (yellow jackets and wasps being the most common stingers on the A.T.) are normally a minor annoyance that varies widely in occurrences from year to year. Most folks hike the entire Trail without being stung once, and the few that are stung usually just say a few choice words and continue hiking. If you do get stung, move on quickly to avoid being stung again. In the case of bee stings, it is also important to remove any stinger still imbedded by scraping it off with a knife blade, taking care not to squeeze the poison sacks that are probably still attached. If you know you have a severe allergic reaction to insect stings, you should seek medical advice about field treatment before you begin your hike.

Snake bites are rare on the A.T. If you watch where you step, your chances of being bitten by a snake are very, very small. Your chances of being bitten by a poisonous snake are even smaller, and, even if poisonous, only about half of those that strike inject venom. In the event venom is injected, you will have pain, redness, and swelling. The best course of action is to remain calm, tie a loose cord around your arm or leg, between the bite and your torso (don't cut off circulation!), and get to a doctor. If you can do so safely, kill the snake for later identification. As for the usefulness of snakebite kits, the experts are still divided. Should you decide to use one, follow its instructions precisely. Avoid the use of alcohol or stimulants.

Giardia lamblia enters your system when you drink water contaminated by infected animals (beavers being the most common culprit, hence the popular nickname, "beaver fever"). Early symptoms include gas, cramps, and diarrhea, and you may at first think you have a simple case of "the runs." Giardia is diarrhea that will not go away in a few days, and you will need to get prescription medication from a doctor to cure it. In the meantime, drink plenty of liquids to avoid dehydration.

Hypothermia results when the body's heat production cannot keep up with heat loss. It usually happens when the air temperature is between 25-45°F, aggravated by conditions of hunger, fatigue, wind, and wetness. Early indications are a general chill, tiredness, and irritability. Definite signs include slurred speech, loss of motor control and upper body strength, lethargy, and convulsive shivering. Rapid warming is the best treatment. Take shelter, remove wet clothes, get into dry clothes and a sleeping bag, and drink hot liquids.

Heat exhaustion occurs when the body's cooling system overloads. So much blood goes to the skin that internal organs are deprived. Early signs include faintness and nausea. You will sweat profusely, your skin will feel strangely cool, and your face will be pale. Fortunately, you will not feel like hiking anymore, and that is good. Seek shade and lay down. Loosen or remove some clothing. Sip on lightly salted water or an electrolyte-replacement drink. In half-an-hour, you will be able to resume your trek-at a more leisurely pace, of course.

Heat stroke is life-threatening, with symptoms that are very different from those of simple heat exhaustion. You will stop sweating and feel suffocatingly hot. Your skin will feel hot and be very dry to the touch, and you may be on the verge of losing consciousness. Immediate cooling is the only treatment. If you can, lay down in a stream or lake, or pour water over your body. If you are with companions, ask them to massage your arms and legs to increase blood flow. Once you have recovered sufficiently, leave the Trail, and seek immediate medical treatment.

Lightning should be considered a real danger on the Trail. If you are caught in a thunderstorm on a mountaintop or ridge, get to a lower elevation if there is time, or take cover among same-sized boulders if not. If in an exposed meadow, take cover among the surrounding trees if there is time, or crouch down if not. If possible, insulate yourself with a sleeping pad or other nonconducting object, but do not lie flat. Get away from your pack and other metal objects. In general, avoid prominent rocks, cliffs, and the tallest trees. Try not to be, or be near, the highest point in your vicinity.

Hygiene

Staying clean on a long hike is not as hard as you may imagine. A sponge bath every day is possible if you can stand the cold water. Some thru-hikers take a collapsible bowl for bathing, but a water bag and bandanna do just fine for most people. Bathing and washing hair should be done away from water sources, of course. When bathing with water is not possible, baby powder or bath powder makes a satisfactory substitute, but not for long. Dental care is the same as at home, except that it is easy to neglect flossing and brushing teeth when tired or when the weather is bad. As for waste disposal, you will need toilet paper and matches, both carried in a waterproof plastic bag. A plastic trowel for digging cat holes is optional, since most hikers find that their boot heels are sufficient digging tools. Women thru-hikers handle their special hygiene needs as they would on any trip, noting that tampons and sanitary napkins, which are nondegradable, should not be disposed of in privies or buried in the woods, so pack extra Ziploc-type bags for packing them out. Some women stop having a monthly menstrual cycle during the latter part of their hike due to the increased physical activity and decreased percentage of body fat. On the other hand, some women are affected in the opposite way by long-distance hiking. Post-menopausal women often resume having a monthly flow. These conditions are temporary and should not be a cause for undue concern unless accompanied by other symptoms.

Grooming Kit

Your grooming kit should have everything you need to keep you clean, but it does not have to be elaborate. Except for bathing, brushing your teeth, clipping your nails, and perhaps combing your hair, all other grooming functions are optional on the Trail. If underarm odor becomes a noticeable problem (it isn't for most hikers), using deodorant will help keep body odor from permeating your pack straps, and will be appreciated by other hikers. A lightweight towel, drying cloth, or extra bandanna can also be handy. Shaving for both men and women is purely a matter of choice. Whatever standard of grooming you maintain on the Trail, you should always try to present the best possible appearance when going into Trail towns. A grooming kit checklist is provided on page 61.

Laundry

Washing clothes is usually done in Trail towns. You will be able to launder your clothes at a commercial laundromat about once a week on average. You may also need to wash clothing in camp (away from water sources) during hot weather. A large Ziploc-type bag makes an excellent "washing machine," but be careful about using soap when washing in cold water. Soap residue in shorts or shirts can cause painful skin irritation while you are hiking. Never use chlorine bleach when washing nylon or other synthetic clothing, especially socks. If you develop athlete's foot or similar fungal infections, you may want to use a non-chlorine bleach (e.g., Clorox II) to kill any organisms retained in your clothing.

PLANNING STEPS - HEALTH AND HYGIENE

Step 1. Schedule medical and dental checkups. If you have special medical considerations, discuss on-Trail treatment with your doctor.

Step 2. Begin conditioning for your hike, doing long walks on rough terrain if possible, and wearing your fully-loaded pack (loaded with simulated weight until you have all of your gear). Focus on toughening your feet.

Step 3. Assemble a first-aid kit that will suit your special needs. A first-aid kit checklist in illustrated on page 61 to assist you.

Step 4. Assemble a grooming kit that will suit your special needs. A grooming kit checklist is illustrated on page 61 to assist you.

Step 5. Obtain a medical bracelet for wearing on the Trail if you have any allergies to medicines or have special medical problems, such as diabetes. If you use special medications, write instructions for using them on the container, in case of an emergency situation requiring a fellow hiker to administer medication.

Step 6. Check your medical insurance, and have a copy of your insurance card made for carrying on your hike.

7

Scheduling and Maildrops

The average thru-hiker finds that scheduling and maildrops are perhaps the most difficult parts of a thru-hike to plan—or at least they take the most work. This chapter simplifies the process for you. It shows you how to draft a daily hiking schedule and how to select maildrop locations. You will need the *Data Book* for drafting your hiking schedule and the *Handbook* for selecting maildrop locations. The current year's editions of both publications may be used for planning purposes, but your final plans should be verified against and updated with information from the editions published for the year you are doing your hike.

Preliminary Considerations

Some thru-hikers prefer to do no scheduling before their hikes, feeling that this lack of prehike scheduling allows them greater flexibility and spontaneity once they are on the Trail. They plan their itinerary week by week, calculating at each town stop the number of days to their next resupply point and the food they will need to reach it. This method of "non-scheduling" is suitable if you have unlimited time for doing your hike and do not plan to use maildrops as your method of resupplying. Even if you choose to do no prehike scheduling, however, know that you will still do the same overall amount of scheduling as those who do prehike scheduling, the only difference being that you will do it piecemeal while you are underway. If you must do your thru-hike within a specified time frame and/or want to use maildrops for resupplying, either partially or totally, you will definitely need to draft a prehike schedule. It will be impossible to exactly follow this schedule once you begin your hike, but it has great value as a planning tool, and, if done properly, leaves plenty of room for spontaneity once you are underway. You can begin drafting a daily schedule for your entire trip as soon as you have decided on a date for beginning your hike, chosen which direction you will travel, selected a target date for finishing, and have obtained your *Data Book*.

Direction of Travel

You can do your thru-hike in one of two directions—either south to north or north to south—or you can use a combination of the two called "flip-flopping." Each year, between 1,500 and 2,000 people choose to travel from Georgia to Maine. Another 100 to 200 individuals choose to go in the opposite direction. A few dozen will flip-flop. The following points can help you decide which is best for you:
• *South to north:* If you start your hike in Georgia, you can begin early in the year. Most of the bitter winter weather is over in the South by late March. You may still encounter occasional days and nights with freezing temperatures, and possibly some snow at the higher elevations as late as May, but, for the most part, you will be following the progression of spring northward. You will be in the main flow of thru-hikers, meaning businesses and facilities that cater to hikers will be open. You will also be part of the traditional thru-hiker social scene. On the northern end, you will miss the blackfly season (June-August) and catch the foliage season in New England (late September).
• *North to south:* If you begin in Maine, you must wait until late May or early June to begin, and there may still be snow on the ground in some places at the higher elevations. Blackflies and bogs may be bad in Maine, and streams will occasionally be raging because of the snow melt and spring rains. Early vacation crowds may be overrunning the White Mountains in New Hampshire. Water in springs from New York to Virginia may be flowing slowly in late summer, and late-summer growth can be rampant in the southern Appalachians. Ice and snow are almost certain in the southern Appalachians and Smokies. Finally, you can end up in Georgia during the October-November hunting season. However, you can have a more solitary hike by going against the flow, especially in the final stages of your hike after the warm-weather hikers have disappeared. Few southbounders encounter all of the possible problems mentioned above, and most seem to enjoy their hikes to the same degree as northbounders.

- *Flip-flopping:* Flip-flopping is a method of thru-hiking that involves beginning your hike at one terminus, hiking toward the other terminus for perhaps half the distance of the Trail, jumping ahead to the other terminus, then hiking back toward the initial terminus to finish at the point where you jumped. A variation is to begin near the midpoint of the Trail (perhaps Harpers Ferry, West Virginia), hike to one terminus, then travel to the other terminus and hike back to the midpoint where you began. Flip-flopping is attractive to those who must start their hikes late in the spring, perhaps after school is out. Northbounders who fall considerably behind their planned schedule, and fear getting caught by winter weather in New England, often flip-flop. Southbounders rarely feel the need to do so.

Starting Date

Most northbounders start from Georgia in late March or April, with the greatest concentration of thru-hikers starting on weekends in early April. To do a normal northbound thru-hike, you should start no later than the early part of May if you expect to reach Katahdin before it possibly closes due to weather (see below). Most southbounders choose to start from Maine after June 1. There is no perfect starting date for either northbounders or southbounders, since weather and crowds vary without rhyme or reason from year to year on both ends of the Trail, so, within the normal range of starting dates mentioned earlier in this paragraph, pick a starting date that is best for your own circumstances and go with it for planning purposes.

Finishing Date

If you go south to north, you should plan on finishing your hike before October 15, the date that rangers officially close Maine's Baxter State Park to the public. If you try to finish later in October, you will be taking a chance that Katahdin may be iced over and closed to climbing, according to weather records. In past years, some unfortunate northbounders have been forced to end their hikes at Katahdin Stream Campground, five miles short of Baxter Peak, unable to reach the terminus sign on top. If you go north to south, you are not limited by any such closing date on Springer, but weather in the southern Appalachians and Smokies can be severe in late November and December. In either case, you should set a target date for finishing your hike. You may have to change it later in your hike, but for now you will need it for planning your schedule.

Average Daily Mileage

It is important for planning purposes to know the average-miles-per-day figure that you will need in order to complete your hike in the amount of time you have available. After you have selected a starting date and a target finishing date, calculate from a calendar the total number of days available for doing your thru-hike. Use the number of available days in the formula below to calculate the average-miles-per-day figure needed for planning your hike.

$$1.2 \times (2{,}150 \text{ miles} \div \text{number of available days}) = _____ \text{ miles per day}$$

The formula takes into account the hiking time you lose while staying over in towns, taking rest breaks on the Trail, *etc.*, and will be of great help in drafting your daily schedule. However, keep in mind that this average-miles-per-day figure is, at best, an approximation. Use it as a planning tool, but never try to use it as a rule for hiking once you are on the Trail.

Scheduling

Now that you have selected starting and finishing dates, calculated the average-miles-per-day figure needed to complete your hike on time, and obtained your *Data Book*, you can begin drafting a schedule for your hike. Remember that this schedule will be used primarily for planning purposes before your hike. You should be careful in its preparation, but no real harm is done if you make small errors here and there. Also keep in mind that it will be impossible to exactly follow this schedule once you begin your hike. You will be able to follow it loosely, and will probably want to do so, but adjustments will have to be made from time to time as you go along and circumstances change during your hike. Nevertheless, this prehike schedule has great value as a tool for ensuring that your plans fit within the time limits for your hike, selecting your maildrops, predicting with some accuracy the food and supplies that should be sent to each maildrop location, and estimating expenses during your hike. Instructions and advice for drafting your schedule are given below, and a sample hiking schedule for a complete thru-hike is shown on pages 67-72 to assist you. You should carefully study the sample schedule before you proceed with the discussion and instructions that follow.

How to Draft a Hiking Schedule

The scheduling method described in this section is built around the premise that, during each day of your journey, you must spend the night somewhere, either in a shelter or tent on the Trail, or in a Trail town. Each overnight stop, called a "destination" on the sample scheduling form, comes at the end of a numbered day (indicated by "day #"). Notice that a destination is reached after hiking the mileage figure shown to its left, and that each day number will have a corresponding date, day of the week, mileage figure (which will be zero if you aren't hiking that day), and destination where you will spend the night. For the time being, ignore the columns at the far right of the scheduling form marked MD#, B, L, and S. These columns will be used later for recording maildrop locations and meal sources.

Step S1: Using your first scheduling page and *Data Book*, fill in the information for your first day of hiking, which becomes day number one of your hike. In the example shown on page 67, the information for the first day reads: "On day number one of my hike, April 4, a Wednesday, I plan to hike 8.9 miles to the Springer Mountain Shelter, where I will stay overnight." Keep in mind that you will have a destination for every day of your trip, even if you do no hiking.

Step S2: After entering information for the first day, use the *Data Book* to select destinations for the next few days that require only moderate mileage figures, perhaps even going from shelter to shelter. The mileage figures selected during this period will be lower than the average-miles-per-day amount. Include stops for resupplying as often as possible in this early part of your schedule, to keep your food weight to a minimum. Northbounders can resupply at either Suches or Neels Gap, Georgia, during the first week. Southbounders will have to carry a big load through the 100-mile wilderness between Abol Bridge and Monson, Maine.

Step S3: After a week or two of lower mileage figures, to allow your body to adjust to daily hiking, begin raising your daily mileage figures to the average-miles-per day amount that you calculated above. This does not mean that you must hike exactly that mileage figure each day. You may fall below it by a few miles one day and exceed it by several miles the next day, depending on the destinations you choose. The idea is to have the mileage figures you pick average the same (or slightly above) the average-miles-per-day amount you calculated as necessary for your entire hike. Again, do not forget to include stops for resupplying.

Step S4: Once your daily mileage figures are averaging the same or higher than the average-miles-per-day amount, you can continue scheduling in two ways (or a combination of the two), each of which will automatically select the towns you will use for resupplying:
• *Scheduling by town stops:* You can begin planning ahead from one town stop to the next, picking which Trail towns you want to visit. Using your *Data Book* for mileage figures, calculate the total distance in miles between the last town you scheduled for a visit and the next town you would like to visit. Divide that total distance by the average-miles-per-day amount to determine how many overnight stops you will need on the Trail between the two town stops. Remember that each day of hiking is a day of food weight, so do not schedule more days between towns than you can carry food. Add the required number of day numbers to the scheduling form (and, if you want, select a destination for each day from your *Data Book* and enter it by name), then go on to the next town stop, calculating the number of overnight stops required between towns in the same manner. Do not forget to record the days on which you do no hiking as day numbers and destinations on your scheduling form.
• *Scheduling by food weight:* You can let your town stops be determined by the number of days of food (i.e., weight) you want to carry between town stops. Using this method, multiply the number of days of food you

Scheduling and Maildrops

want to carry by the average-miles-per-day amount to get a total mileage figure for that segment of your hike. Using the *Data Book*, add that total mileage figure to the mileage figure for your last town stop, selecting the town listed closest to the resulting total mileage figure as your next town stop. Again, do not forget to record the days on which you do no hiking as day numbers and destinations on your scheduling form.

Note: As you consider town stops for resupplying, check to ensure that you are not expecting to pick up maildrops when post offices are closed (usually Saturday afternoons, Sundays, and holidays; see "Post Office Information" on pages 83-84). You should also verify from the "Table of Town Services" on pages 85-86 and the *Handbook* that the towns you have selected for resupplying have all of the services you will need, and, if not, pick alternate maildrop locations.

Step S5: Whichever of the two ways you use to continue scheduling the remainder of your hike, you will want to consider the following scheduling adjustments which have been recommended by many thru-hikers:
- Schedule overnight town stops regularly, even if you are not using maildrops or your preference is to stay in the woods as much as possible and drop into towns only briefly to resupply. Most thru-hikers need an occasional break from the woods and find that an overnight town stay refreshes them both mentally and physically.
- Schedule a short hiking day into a town, stay overnight, and schedule a short hiking day out. This plan allows you a full 24 hours in town, which is normally more than enough time to get everything done and to rest as well, without breaking your hiking rhythm.
- Schedule days of varying length, with longer days toward the end of a section (when your pack is lighter), and schedule some no-hiking days occasionally. For example, a typical section might be: short day out of town, average day, average day, long day, long day, short day into town, day off in town.
- Schedule some two-day, or even three-day, breaks along the way, perhaps at Hot Springs, North Carolina; Damascus, Virginia; Delaware Water Gap, Pennsylvania; Hanover, New Hampshire; and Monson, Maine. These long breaks will allow your body to rest and relax to a degree that is not possible on an overnight stop. Long stops are also good opportunities to examine and repair equipment.
- Schedule somewhat shorter days through the rocks of Pennsylvania (Duncannon to Delaware Water Gap, although, if you have strong ankles and legs, you may not be slowed down very much), the White Mountains of New Hampshire (Glencliff to Gorham), and the Mahoosucs of Maine (Gorham to Stratton). You will beat yourself to death if you try to maintain twenty-mile days through these sections.
- Do not count on being able to use the AMC (Appalachian Mountain Club) huts through the White Mountains. You may be able to get a reservation by calling ahead, or by working for room and board, but the AMC hut-reservation system is not really geared for thru-hikers, whose itinerary is usually somewhat indeterminate. For scheduling purposes, count on using the designated AMC campsites and shelters (noted as such in the *Data Book*) through the Whites. You can always make different arrangements when you get to the AMC area and have access to more information and have a better idea of your hiking abilities.
- Schedule higher mileage figures through the Shenandoah National Park and Great Smoky Mountains National Park if you wish. The Trail through both is relatively easy, although it is a shame to rush through these beautiful parks. Camping, except at designated shelters or campsites, is restricted in both parks.

Step S6: Continue to work on your basic schedule until you have one that shows reasonable mileage figures for each hiking day, includes sufficient maildrops and town breaks, and fits within your starting and finishing dates. While you are making scheduling adjustments, you may want to check your daily plans against the map profiles to ensure that you have not scheduled a high-mileage day in difficult terrain, and, if you have, adjust your mileage figures downward.

Step S7: Once you have finalized your schedule, you can number your maildrop locations in the "MD#" column on your scheduling forms. You can also determine the source of each meal you will eat on your hike and the meals that should be packed for each maildrop location. This latter part is accomplished by filling in the B, L, and S columns on the scheduling forms as discussed in Chapter 5 (see instructions given in the "Calculating Food Quantities" section on page 35).

Several drafts of your hiking schedule will probably be necessary before everything fits into its proper place, especially if your first attempt has you finishing later than your target finishing date, so use a pencil. Scheduling can be exasperating at first, but the effort you put into prehike scheduling is worth it. As you work to make all the pieces mesh, you will gain valuable insights about the facilities along the Trail and in towns, and you will get a preview of how you will operate from day to day once you are on the Trail. The scheduling expertise you gain while drafting your prehike schedule will also prove invaluable when you need to make on-the-spot adjustments to your schedule during your hike, as you most certainly will.

Maildrops

The number of maildrops you plan to use for resupplying will be determined by how many towns you want to visit during your hike, the food weight you want to carry between town stops, and/or the pace at which you plan to do your hike. Obviously, by carrying more food weight and hiking more miles each day, you will be able to go farther between stops and use fewer maildrops. Having a small number of maildrops is not of prime concern, however, and there is no need to carry huge food loads on the A.T. unless you enjoy suffering. A compromise between the number of maildrops and total pack weight is best. Most thru-hikers carry 5-10 days of food (weighing 10-25 pounds), which allows them to hike 75-150 miles without resupplying. Most use a total of 15-25 maildrops. Your plans should fall within these ranges.

A list of frequently used post offices is provided on pages 83-84, and you should select your maildrop locations from this list. The post offices in these towns will hold packages almost indefinitely (unless noted otherwise), whereas post offices unaccustomed to dealing with hiker mail may send your maildrop package back home after fifteen days. It is also good to pick post offices in towns that have other vital services, such as a hostel or motel, grocery store or supermarket, laundromat, and stove-fuel source. You can consult the "Table of Town Services" on pages 85-86 for basic information about services in Trail towns, with full information about thru-hiker services available in the *Handbook*. It is easiest to pick maildrops as you are doing scheduling, as described in the scheduling instructions. When you select a town as a maildrop location, you should put its number in the "MD#" column on the scheduling form, numbering your maildrops in the sequence that they occur on the form. Once you have finalized your selection of maildrops on your hiking schedule, you should:
- List each maildrop in order by number and location on your maildrop packing lists.
- List each maildrop by number, location, and ZIP Code on a maildrop posting schedule (see sample illustrated on page 79), together with your due date for arriving at that location.

To calculate the date for mailing a maildrop package to a post office, use a calendar to find a date that allows a minimum of ten to fourteen post-office working days before you expect to arrive at the post office. Record the date you select in the mailing-date column on your maildrop posting schedule. Be sure to compensate for holidays and weekends when calculating the mailing date. You should carry a copy of your maildrop posting schedule with you on your hike, or record the information in your *Data Book* or *Handbook* for quick reference on the Trail.

Packaging and Labeling

The boxes discarded by beverage stores are sturdily made to protect glass contents, and make excellent maildrop boxes. Avoid thin cardboard boxes. Use a 2-inch plastic wrapping tape (avoid duct tape) and wrap tape completely around each box in several directions. Use a self-adhesive label, printed or typed clearly as follows:

> Your Name
> c/o General Delivery
> City, State, ZIP Code

Place the phrase "Hold for A.T. hiker" and your expected due date in the lower corner of the box or label. You may want to write your last name, destination of the maildrop, and ZIP Code elsewhere on the box, just in case the label detaches. The U.S. Postal Service rarely loses maildrop packages that are properly wrapped and addressed, so take the time necessary to do a good job. **Important:** Do not send UPS or Federal Express packages to post offices, since postal personnel are prevented by law from accepting and/or holding them.

PLANNING STEPS - SCHEDULING AND MAILDROPS

Step 1. Decide your direction of travel, either south to north or north to south (or flip-flopping).

Step 2. Decide on a starting date and pick a target finishing date.

Step 3. Calculate the average daily mileage figure for your hike, based on your starting and finishing dates.

Step 4. Study the sample hiking schedule shown in the "Sample Planning Notebook" section on pages 67-72, noting the manner in which information is recorded.

Step 5. Draft your hiking schedule, using the blank forms in the workbook section and following the instructions outlined in the "How to Draft a Hiking Schedule" section of this chapter.

Step 6. Number the maildrop locations on your scheduling forms. Also list these maildrop numbers and locations on each of your maildrop packing lists.

Step 7. Prepare a maildrop posting schedule as described in the discussion on maildrops in this chapter, and calculate the dates for mailing each maildrop.

Step 8. Use your hiking schedule to determine the quantity of meals (breakfasts, lunches, and suppers) you will need for each maildrop location, and use this information to complete your food preparations (see "Calculating Food Quantities" on page 35).

Step 9. Make a copy of your hiking schedule and your maildrop posting schedule for carrying with you during your hike, or transfer the information to your *Data Book* or *Handbook* for quick reference on the Trail.

8

Budgeting and Finances

A thru-hike is not a terribly expensive journey, but it does take money. As was pointed out earlier in this guide, you will need a minimum of $2,200 (a dollar a mile) for a "normal" thru-hike, assuming you have already purchased your equipment, some of your food, and not taking into account your travel expenses to and from the Trailheads. For that amount, you can do a very fine hike. If you choose to do a more Spartan trip with fewer overnight town stops, you can budget a bit more modestly. If you elect to visit many towns, stay in motels rather than hostels, and eat often at restaurants, your expenses will be considerably greater. Most first-time thru-hikers end up spending more than the amount indicated above, usually between $3,000 and $4,000, because they choose to take more time off in towns and have bigger restaurant appetites than anticipated. Other common unanticipated expenses include purchases of gear and medical expenses.

Trail Towns

Thru-hikers joke that Trail towns should have one machine on the edge of town that takes all of their money as they enter and another that gives receipts as they leave, because towns seem to literally eat money, often in big gulps. The amount you spend is up to you, of course, but certain expenses are hard to avoid. You will need overnight lodging, which usually means staying in a hostel, motel, hotel, or bed-and-breakfast inn. Hostels are often free of charge for the first night, and other lodging facilities in Trail towns, especially the smaller towns, are inexpensive compared to the rates you probably pay when traveling by automobile. Most towns have inexpensive places to eat, but you may surprise yourself by the appetite you have when so many culinary temptations are close at hand. Grocery stores and supermarkets add to the expense, normally accounting for the biggest part of your town expenditures. Other town expenses can include packaging and postage for mailing letters and excess gear, calls to the folks back home (a telephone credit card greatly simplifies long-distance calling), detergent and fees for doing laundry, over-the-counter or prescription medicines, grooming supplies, shuttle fees to, from, and around town, and admission fees for entertainment.

Budgeting for On-Trail Expenses

The biggest budgeting challenge for thru-hikers, besides saving enough money to do the trip in the first place, is figuring how much money they will need at each location. A budget planner (see illustration on page 81), together with your hiking schedule, list of accommodations, and a little guesswork, will allow you to estimate the expense money you will need at each resupply location, as follows:

• You can calculate the money you will need for the cost of meals from grocery stores and restaurants by using your hiking schedule, once you have filled in the B, L, and S columns. By assigning an estimated cost for each such meal (perhaps $4 per breakfast, $3 per lunch, and $5 per supper from grocery stores; $5 per breakfast, $5 per lunch, and $8 per supper from restaurants), you can calculate the total cost of meals to be included in each maildrop. Meals included with price of lodging should not be included.

• You can calculate the money you will need for lodging by using your list of accommodations and the *Handbook*, which will give you prices and fees for hostels, motels, hotels, campsites, *etc*. By multiplying the price per day times the number of days you plan to stay, you can estimate the total cost for accommodations to be included in each maildrop.

• You can guess at the miscellaneous expenses (postage, laundry, *etc*.) and "fun money" (for ice cream, pizza, other food items not included in meal plans, entertainment, *etc*.) needed for each location. Postage usually averages about $3 per town stop; laundry (washing, drying, detergent) about $2.50 per load.

Once you have filled in the basic information, you can calculate on your budget planner the total amount of money needed at each maildrop location by adding the individual expenses. Notice that meals from grocery stores and restaurants are recorded as a dollar amount, arrived at by multiplying the number of meals by the cost per meal that you think you will spend. As you do your calculations, keep in mind that the money must be sent to the resupply location (*i.e.,* included in the maildrop package) prior to the locations where you will spend the money.

Costs of Accommodations

Accommodations can be listed, and the total cost of lodging to be included in each maildrop location can be calculated, as soon as you have completed your hiking schedule and know which towns and fee-charging campsites you plan to be using during your hike. A sample list of accommodations is provided on page 80 to assist you. You will need a copy of the *Handbook* for detailed information about fees at hostels and public accommodations in towns along the Trail, and for information about camping fees charged by facilities on the Trail. Keep in mind that your cost calculations are only approximations and will certainly change as your hike progresses.

Carrying and Obtaining Money

You should avoid hiking with large amounts of cash on your person, primarily for your own peace of mind. There are safer ways to carry funds on a thru-hike and convenient ways to obtain money as you go along, with most thru-hikers using one or more of the following methods:

• *Traveler's checks* purchased before you start your hike are the easiest and safest way to carry funds on the Trail, and most thru-hikers rely on them for financing their hikes *en route*. All businesses on or near the A.T. accept traveler's checks, but you should avoid large denominations since smaller facilities may not have enough cash on hand to give change. Most thru-hikers carry the $20 denomination and have few problems. You can include traveler's checks in your maildrops, but plan to have a backup supply with you at all times in case your maildrop is delayed or missing when you get to town. If you lose your traveler's checks, you can arrange to have them replaced by telephone but may have to go some distance off the Trail to obtain replacements.

• *ATM cards* can be used to obtain money in some locations, but not in most small towns and communities on or near the Trail, so you should verify locations before you leave if you plan to use this method of obtaining money on a regular basis. Most thru-hikers rely on their ATM cards only to supplement their supply of traveler's checks.

• *Credit cards* are handy if you have to order equipment from the Trail, and are accepted at many facilities for food and lodging as noted in the *Handbook*. They can also be used to obtain cash advances from ATM machines in locations along the Trail that have ATM networks.

• *Postal money orders* are used by some thru-hikers but have disadvantages. Small post offices often keep minimum amounts of cash on hand. If you must use them, plan to call ahead to make arrangements if you expect to cash a large postal money order, and plan to have a photo I.D. ready. If you are having money sent from home by money order, it may be a good idea to have your benefactor send several money orders of a smaller amount instead of one large order.

• *Western Union* facilities are available in some Trail towns, as noted in the *Handbook*, in case you need money fast, but few thru-hikers use this method except in case of an emergency.

Funds for use during you hike can be allotted for shipment in several ways if you are using traveler's checks. The amount you need for each location can be included in each maildrop package, which has the advantage of keeping you from spending more than you have budgeted for any particular town stop. This method is very useful for those of you, like your author, who tend to overspend if you have "excess" money in your pockets. If you are better disciplined, a larger amount to cover expenses for a number of town stops can be included in a fewer number of maildrop packages. Either way is fine. You may even choose to carry all of your funds with you from the start of your hike, but remember that the weight of 110 or more traveler's checks is considerable. Little money is needed on the footpath itself (bears do not accept cash handouts, even in national parks!), although you may want to take a short side trip to a small grocery store for a soda, snack, or pint of ice cream on occasion, so you should plan to have at least a few dollars in cash and a small-denomination traveler's check in your pack while hiking between towns. You should also have a few quarters with you at all times, for making emergency telephone calls.

PLANNING STEPS - BUDGETING AND FINANCES

Step 1. Use your hiking schedule to calculate the number of breakfasts, lunches, and suppers from grocery stores and restaurants that you will need between resupply locations, and record these calculations on your budget planner (see sample budget planner on pages 81).

Step 2. Multiply the number of meals calculated in step 1 by the dollar figure you have assigned for each meal category (see recommended cost-per-meal in the discussion section), and record the total cost for each meal category at each resupply location, being careful to record these total dollar amounts on your budget planner at the resupply location immediately prior to where you will need them.

Step 3. Estimate the miscellaneous expenses and "fun money" you will need between resupply locations, and record the dollar amounts on your budget planner, being careful to record these total dollar amounts on your budget planner at the resupply location immediately prior to where you will need them.

Step 4. Use your list of accommodations and *Handbook* to calculate the cost of lodging at each resupply location, and record the dollar amounts on your budget planner, being careful to record these dollar amounts on your budget planner at the resupply location immediately prior to where you will need them.

Step 5. Tally the cost of meals, miscellaneous expenses, "fun money," and accommodations to show the total amount of expense money you will need at each resupply location during your hike.

Step 6. Decide on the method of carrying the funds you will need during your hike, and select a method for sending these funds to yourself. If you are including funds in maildrops, choose an allotment method (exact amount in every maildrop, large amount in a few maildrops, *etc.*) Package funds in a sealed envelope inside a Ziploc-type bag for protection from food items and moisture during shipment.

Step 7. Make a list of the amount of money you are packing in each maildrop for carrying with you during your hike, or record the information in your *Data Book* or *Handbook* for ready reference on the Trail.

Step 8. Check expiration dates on credit cards. If you are not taking credit cards, consider placing a few blank personal checks in each maildrop in case of emergency.

9

Miscellaneous Topics

Most thru-hikers have a catchall bag in which they carry useful items that do not seem to fit anywhere else. This chapter serves the same purpose in this guide. The topics discussed are no less important than those discussed in other chapters but may not be needed by every hiker. Planning steps are not included at the end of this chapter, so you should take note of any planning actions that apply to your situation as you read the discussions, adding them to your "Things to Do" sheet if you are using a planning notebook.

Hiking with a Partner

Partners are like backpacks. Having the right one makes a thru-hike so much more enjoyable, but having the wrong one will be a constant irritation. Most thru-hikers start their hikes without a partner and, after they have been on the Trail for awhile, discover that they enjoy the freedom of not having a permanent companion, preferring the company of many short-term partners instead. Few thru-hikers who begin their hikes with a partner will finish with the same partner. The main reason most partnerships dissolve is that the two partners hike differently. Many partners who are wonderful friends back home, and even on weekend hikes, find that their hiking paces and interests are not compatible on a long hike. Trying to cope with differing paces and dissimilar interests for twenty-four hours, day after day, can test the best of friendships. Small irritations that would normally be overlooked become major contentions under the stress. Even some happily married couples have had hiking-compatibility problems on a thru-hike.

Despite the difficulties of finding a compatible partner, there are some good reasons for seeking one. Safety is probably the most important. Should you have a serious illness or accident, your partner can go for help. Another is lowered pack weight. By sharing tent, stove, cooking gear, water filter, and other gear, both partners carry less total weight. Of course, the best reason is that the right partner can add the dimension of shared enjoyment. ATC members can advertise for a partner in the *Appalachian Trailway News* at no cost, and the Center for Appalachian Trail Studies has a free listing of people seeking a partner for a thru-hike (include a stamped, self-addressed envelope with your request). Many a friendship has begun this way, even if the partnership did not work out on the Trail.

If you plan to hike the A.T. with a stranger, both of you should verify, by hiking together beforehand if possible, that you have similar hiking paces and Trail interests. In addition, you should agree on goals for your hike and discuss beforehand how to handle differences that may occur. Each of you should be realistic about the chances against having a partnership that will go the distance, and each partner should have back-up equipment available at home if one of you later decides to go it alone or leave the Trail. If you begin your hike alone and gain a partner in the early part of your hike, the chances of this partnership going the remainder of the distance are somewhat better than for prearranged partnerships. For one thing, both you and your newly found partner will probably have compatible hiking paces and styles, factors that make it possible for the two of you to meet often enough on the Trail to become acquainted and consider being partners in the first place. Working against the partnership is the fact that you will not have the bonds of long-term friendship to see you through the periods of stress.

Hiking with a Group

Environmentalist and Trail organizations request that you keep group travel on the A.T. to ten persons or less. This is not a hardship on most thru-hikers. They rarely choose to travel in large groups, since the dynamics of such groups tend to diminish the thru-hiking experience for all of the individuals concerned. Some thru-hikers do begin their hikes as part of a small group or later form into small informal groups on the Trail, usually for brief periods.

Hiking with a Child

Hiking with a young child can be a joy, but not on a thru-hike. A few children have hiked long distances on the A.T. with their parents, but reportedly none have really enjoyed the experience. Children simply do not have the emotional reserves necessary to cope with the constant change (people, places, weather, *etc.*) inherent in thru-hiking. Plus, they miss being with kids their own age. Someone who saw thru-hiking parents struggling up the Trail with a two-year-old child wisely observed that "no one should be doing a thru-hike unless they are doing so of their own volition and for their own reasons." If you are considering taking your child (under fourteen or fifteen years of age) on a thru-hike, you are to be commended for your desire to introduce him or her to the outdoors, but wisdom says to do so on shorter trips.

Hiking with a Dog

Hiking with a dog is often rewarding for the owner, but there are problems that must be faced on a thru-hike. For starters, your dog cannot hike the entire Trail. Great Smoky Mountains National Park and Baxter State Park do not allow dogs, an absolute prohibition vigorously enforced to protect wildlife. Stiff fines are levied on offending owners. Shenandoah National Park, and many state and local parks through which the Trail passes require that dogs be on a leash at all times, even while hiking. In towns, many hostels and public accommodations will not allow dogs inside, and in camp most of your fellow thru-hikers prefer not to have dogs on the sleeping platforms in shelters, especially on a rainy night when gear is easily soiled by a wet animal. Perhaps most important, the journey itself is often too physically demanding for most dogs, with damaged footpads and malnutrition common occurrences. Then there are the possible "close encounters of the disastrous kind" with wildlife. Thru-hikers place their animals in danger of being bitten by poisonous snakes when they roam off the footpath, quilled by porcupines, sprayed by skunks, or worse. The ATC and many A.T. clubs strongly recommend that you leave your dog at home, and most of your fellow thru-hikers will echo this request, but you are not prohibited from hiking with your pet except in the parks mentioned above.

Note: If you would like practical advice about long-distance hiking with a dog, from a practicing veterinarian who successfully thru-hiked with his dog in 1988 (*i.e.*, successful from the standpoint of himself, the dog, and other thru-hikers), write to: Tom Grennell, V.M.D., 501 W. 4th Street, Roanoke Rapids, North Carolina 27870. Enclose a stamped, self-addressed envelope and he will send you a packet of information, or, if you have questions, call him at (919) 535-1952 between 7 p.m. and 9 p.m., Eastern Time.

Communicating with Family and Friends

Communicating with family and friends from the Trail will not be a problem for you. You can simply pick up a telephone or write a letter from a Trail town. For the ones back home, however, trying to figure how to write someone with a constantly changing address can be confusing. You can help them communicate with you by giving them the list of your planned town stops, with ZIP codes and due dates, before you leave. You will also need to explain the method of addressing general-delivery mail (see example on page xx). Hikers who do this find that many folks will send encouraging notes, goodies, and other tokens of support.

Having Family and Friends Join You

Family and friends will want to share in your adventure, but think twice about having them hike with you unless you are prepared to slow down to their pace. Several weeks after you begin your hike, you will be cranking out the miles with ease. Those who join you will not be toughened to the demands of the Trail, and trying to keep up with you will not be their idea of fun. Many thru-hikers have found that having family and friends join them in Trail towns for dinner and relaxation is a better visit for everyone concerned. Some thru-hikers are also tempted to have family members and/or friends join them for the last week or so of their hikes. This wish to include loved ones is admirable, but you would do well to consider the ramifications very carefully, as follows:

Northbounders finish their hikes in the 100-mile wilderness (Monson to Abol Bridge, Maine), which is one of the most remote sections on the entire Trail. A ten-day supply of food is recommended, quite a burden for possibly out-of-condition hikers. Should your new partner develop problems in this section, requiring extra hiking days, there are no places to resupply, and getting help or leaving the A.T. is difficult. In addition, your attention may be torn between the needs of your new partner, who will not be in tune with the thru-hiker scene, and your fellow thru-hikers, with whom you will feel a great sense of camaraderie after two-thousand miles of shared experience. As for climbing Katahdin itself, keep in mind that it is the single most strenuous climb on the Trail. Most weekend hikers require about four or five hours to ascend to the summit (in ideal weather), and possibly as much time to descend, so it may be best to let family and friends have a party for you and your thru-hiker friends when you descend Katahdin as a new 2,000-Miler, perhaps at Katahdin Stream Campground. You can always stay over in the park or Millinocket and attempt a climb together the next day.

Southbounders often have a different perspective about end-of-hike partners than northbounders. The social ties with other thru-hikers that can be distracting to northbounders are usually less so among southbounders, since, being fewer in number, most travel solo for the majority of their hikes. In addition, their final miles of Trail in Georgia offer more moderate terrain and have good access roads at regular intervals, lessening the chance your new partners will have problems and making it easier to leave the A.T. or get help if they do. The weather is often not ideal, however, since winter is usually closing in by the time southbounders near Springer Mountain. You can have family and friends conveniently drive to meet you for a celebration at Amicalola Falls State Park, Georgia, after you have completed your thru-hike at the Springer Mountain terminus, or they can drive around to Big Stamp Gap on USFS Road 42 and hike the last 0.9 mile to the terminus with you.

Carrying a Wristwatch

Many thru-hikers leave their watches at home, glad to be free from the encumbrance of living on a schedule. A watch has useful functions, however, both on the Trail and in towns. Not the least is the safety factor that it provides by helping you know your location. Once you have been on the Trail for a while, you will be able to tell about how fast you are hiking at any particular time. If you have a watch to tell you how long you have been moving at that pace, you can quite accurately estimate how many miles you have covered and where you are located. This knowledge could prove crucial in an emergency. If you do wear a watch, you can limit its use to the above role if you desire to maintain the illusion that your days are timeless. Mentally, they can be, even if you know the hour. Some watches now offer an altitude reading, and a recent model has a fairly accurate electronic compass that has an LED "needle" with no moving parts.

Taking Photographs

Photography on the Trail is a bother, no matter what equipment you are using. A camera means extra weight in your pack, and you have to stop and remove your pack every time you want to record a scene. Even professional photographers have chafed under the demands of taking photographs under Trail conditions. Most former thru-hikers will tell you, however, that the photos they took on their trips are now among their most treasured keepsakes and that the extra weight and effort was worth it.

If you already have a fine 35mm system that you have been using successfully on other trips, you will probably want to carry it on the Trail. You should be guided by weight as you select which pieces of camera equipment to carry on your hike. Most such thru-hikers limit themselves to one all-purpose zoom lens (moderate wide-angle to moderate telephoto), a flash unit, and perhaps a lightweight tripod. If you are not an experienced photographer, you will probably do better with one of the small, lightweight 35mm automatic-everything (autofocus, autoflash, autowind, *etc.*) cameras. They are easy to carry in a pack, easy to use in difficult conditions, and produce very good results for most amateurs. Many models are water-resistant or even waterproof. Some have zoom capabilities. Disposable models are available if you do not need fine quality. You can protect your camera gear by keeping it in a Ziploc-type bag in your pack, placed among your clothing for padding. A small tabletop tripod (the Ultrapod brand weighs only 2 oz.) will allow you to include yourself in some of your shots if your camera has a self-timer or remote shutter control. Some hikers carrying compact cameras have found it handy to carry it in a small zippered belt pocket during the day, to catch those spontaneous encounters with wildlife.

The decision to use slide film or print film depends on how you plan to use your photos after your hike. If you think you will be sharing your pictures with large groups, slides are the way to go. You can later have prints of your best shots made from slides at most photo outlets. If you will be sharing you pictures mainly with family and friends, prints are easier to use and more personal, and can be displayed in a photo album. Use either 100, 200, or 400 ASA film for best results, with 200 ASA being the film-speed of preference for thru-hikers. The number of photos you take is entirely up to you, with two or three a day being the average. Most thru-hikers record the location and subject of each photograph in their *Data Book* or *Handbook*, or use a small spiral notebook if they are taking many pictures.

Keeping a Journal

Writing down the details of your trip is like taking photos. It is a nuisance but later proves invaluable as a means of recalling the events of your hike. Most thru-hikers use a small notebook for recording their thoughts (some have tried substituting a small tape recorder, but these devices often give erratic performance in humid conditions). Spiral-type notebooks are inexpensive, lightweight, and easy to use in the shelters, where most journal entries are made. Few thru-hikers write in their journals as they hike along during the day. You should keep your journal in a Ziploc-type bag for protection from moisture. *Helpful hint:* Each day, instead of writing a diary entry to yourself, pretend you are writing a letter about your day to someone back home who knows nothing about the Trail. You will be much more descriptive. You will also have an easier time writing letters when you reach town—they will already be written!

Using Trail Registers

Several types of registers are encountered by thru-hikers on the Trail. Official registers are often placed at road crossing by government entities (National Park Service, U.S. Forest Service, *etc.*) for a variety of purposes. The most important to you, as a thru-hiker, is that your register entry allows you to be quickly located should there be an emergency back home—that is, if you have signed the register. Some A.T. clubs place registers in shelters, and these semiofficial registers serve the same purpose. Trail shelters and hostels often have an unofficial register, normally a simple spiral notebook left by a thru-hiker. These thru-hiker registers serve as the "newspaper of the Trail," allowing individuals to communicate their thoughts and impressions to those who follow. You are free to leave one of these unofficial registers if you come to a shelter without one, or the shelter has a full register (which you are usually asked to pack out and return to the owner, whose address is in the front). You may want to include a small spiral notebook in one of your maildrops for leaving somewhere along the A.T. When it is eventually returned, you will have a unique memento of your trip.

Using a Trail Name

Trail nicknames are fun and are used by most thru-hikers, whether they have them before they start their hikes or acquire them once underway. They serve a useful purpose. Often you will meet ten or so thru-hikers named "John" or "Mary" or whatever during the course of a hike, but normally a Trail name will be used by only one individual in any given year. You can pick your own Trail name or risk having others pick a nickname for you, usually one based on some physical idiosyncrasy or hiking characteristic (*e.g.*, "Bigfoot" or "Path Pounder") . You do not have to use a Trail name, of course, but, if you do, you should always sign your real name in shelter registers in addition to your Trail name, in case of an emergency that requires officials to locate you. Refrain from using your Trail name for mailing purposes, to avoid confusing postal personnel who retrieve your maildrop packages by the surname listed on the identification you show them. Partners should also agree to use one name on maildrop packages if sending everything for both partners in a combined package.

Playing Games in Camp

Many thru-hikers begin their hikes with a deck of cards, miniature chess and/or backgammon sets, and other games, thinking they will have plenty of free time for playing them. Most of these items are sent home early in their hikes. Somehow, thru-hiking itself seems to occupy everyone's time and energy. In camp, most people want to relax without doing anything that requires much mental concentration. Spare time in the evening is usually spent in conversation, writing in Trail registers and personal journals, and previewing the next day's travels. *Hackysack* is the one "game" that is the exception, proving as popular among today's hikers as tossing a frisbee was twenty years ago and requiring less space. Many thru-hikers carry a hackysack and use it almost every day to keep limber and have fellowship with other thru-hikers, or for personal amusement (especially if they are watching your author, whose knees and feet have yet to get the hang of it).

Studying Nature

Time invested in the study of nature before your hike will greatly enrich your experience on the Trail. Any library has wildlife books and guides that will provide the information you need to begin your appreciation of nature's creatures. In addition, you may want to learn as you hike. An excellent set of inexpensive, easy-to-use guides for use in the eastern U.S. is available from the Nature Study Guild, Box 972, Berkeley, California 94701; (510) 525-4778. This series of lightweight (less than 2 ounces each) guide-finders has individual pocket-sized volumes about trees, wildflowers, berries, ferns, and animal tracks. You can write or call for a current price list.

Hitchhiking to Towns

Many past thru-hikers report they never hitchhiked anywhere before they did their hikes and felt a little anxious about trying it. The idea of hitchhiking may make you feel apprehensive, too, but hitching is the easiest way to get to towns near the Trail, often saving you many miles of road-walking. Your pack will identify you to the nearby townspeople as a thru-hiker, and it is from these people that you will normally get a ride. If you so desire, you can offer to pay your benefactor, but usually a few stories about your Trail adventures are a more satisfying payment to them. Some thru-hikers have even been invited to dinner or to stay overnight with a town family as a result of a ride. After a few weeks on the Trail, you will feel comfortable about hitching. You can always decline a ride if you do not like the feel of things, and you should not hesitate to do so politely. Rule of thumb: Trust your instincts.

Sex on the Trail

Misconceptions about sexual activity among thru-hikers abound in some circles, especially in the fantasies of some younger male hikers and non-hiking types. Truth is, most thru-hikers exhibit and express virtually no desire for such activity during a thru-hike. The standing joke about sex on the Trail is that, at the end of a strenuous day of long-distance hiking, everyone is too tired and too dirty to be interested. That is not to say that romance does not blossom and liaisons never happen, but usually a good campsite, tasty meal, and relaxed fellowship with Trail friends are more important and satisfying goals to the people who thru-hike. In practice, the thru-hiking community operates as a big family, with men and women thinking of each other primarily as brothers and sisters rather than as potential sexual partners. Most thru-hikers value this sense of "family" above all other aspects of the Trail experience.

10

Last-Minute Preparations

If you are seriously looking at this chapter, your overall plans are made and your thru-hike is close at hand. I know you are now feeling the almost irresistible lure of the Trail. You are also wondering if there is anything you have forgotten to do. Set your mind at ease by using the planning steps listed at the end of the major chapters as a final checklist to ensure that you have considered everything that needs to be done. Also, verify that each item on your "Things to Do" list has been accomplished. In addition, a few last-minute preparations should be completed before you leave home and while you are *en route* to the Trailhead to begin your adventure, as follows:

Step 1. Check your wallet to ensure that it contains a photo I.D. card (usually a driver's license, which should be renewed if it expires before your expected finishing date), next-of-kin notification instructions, medical-insurance card, ATC membership card, tickets for transportation to the Trailhead, traveler's checks, and a little cash.

Step 2. Check your gear to verify that you are leaving home with everything needed for beginning your hike. In the past, some very excited thru-hikers have arrived at Amicalola Falls without such essentials as their boots. Fill your fuel bottle, unless your transportation to the Trailhead prohibits travel with fuel, and check the freshness of batteries in your flashlight, radio, and camera equipment.

Step 3. Record in your *Data Book* or *Handbook* the names, addresses, and telephone numbers of people you may want to write or call during your hike.

Step 4. Make copies of sales receipts for your major items of equipment (boots, pack, tents, *etc.*) for carrying with you, in case you have to apply for warranty repair or replacement during you hike.

Step 5. Leave a copy of your hiking schedule, maildrop posting schedule, and list of back-up gear with the helper who will send packages and back-up items to you during your hike.

Step 6. Verify your travel arrangements if you are using public conveyances (see the "Travel to the Trailheads" section in the *Handbook*). Take some simple precautions to ensure that your pack arrives with you:
• When traveling by air, have the airline put your pack in a protective box. You may have to ask for this service, but it is provided free on most airlines.
• When traveling by bus, pick a seat over the baggage doors and watch that your pack is not removed when the bus makes stops. When changing from one bus to another, watch to ensure that your pack has been placed on the bus you are boarding. This is a slight hassle, but lost packs are rarely recovered.
• When traveling to Gainesville, *Georgia*, make sure that your pack is not tagged for Gainesville, *Florida*.

Step 7. Read the "Traditions and Practices" section in the *Handbook* before you leave and again while *en route* to the Trailhead. It contains important information and will help you anticipate life on the Trail.

Above all, accept the fact that, no matter how well you have made your plans, everything will not go the way you have planned. Real adventures never do, and that is what makes an end-to-end hike so stimulating and enjoyable. Knowing this, be confident that you can handle the challenges that come your way, relying on your ability to adapt. Welcome the surprises of the Trail as a chance to be creative and to grow. Resolve to make the most of every day, and...

HAVE A GREAT HIKE!

Sample Planning Notebook

Many past thru-hikers have found it valuable to study a finished set of plans for a thru-hike—to see by example how information for the various parts should be recorded and grouped together for later use when you begin buying and assembling the equipment, clothing, food, maildrop contents, and other physical components for doing your hike. This section reproduces the complete planning notebook used for one of your author's past thru-hikes, and it contains the planning forms showing all of the information needed for doing that hike.

The planning forms shown in this section are given only as examples of how you can record and organize the details of your hike. Do not copy the planning details shown on these forms. They worked fine for me, but may not be right for you, and some of the information about the Trail shown on thses forms is already out of date. Make your plans based on your own specific hiking capabilities and preferences, using current information from the latest guides. As you study the individual planning forms illustrated in this section, keep in mind that the following personal considerations governed the way I made my plans:

- I wanted to keep my total pack weight with food and water below about forty-two pounds, a weight determined by my physical size (128lbs., 5'6").
- I wanted to (actually, had to) keep my on-Trail expenses to about $2,000.
- I wanted to start in Georgia and chose to start on April 4 simply because I figured the weather would be spring-like and could get a free ride to the Trailhead that date.
- I wanted to finish around October 1, and calculated that I would need to average about 14 miles per day for my hike.
- I was able to start my hike with fewer cold-weather clothing items than normal because of a very warm spring season in Georgia that year.
- I decided to use maildrops as my primary means of resupply, including basic meal components and supplies in each maildrop along with Traveler's checks for financing my trip.
- I decided to use a few basic meal menus for the entire hike, buying food in bulk at home before my trip, and planned to supplement these meals with food items purchased from grocery stores in Trail towns.

Workbook Section

A blank set of planning forms, identical to the ones illustrated in this section,
is provided for your use in the "Workbook Section" at the end of this guide.

The Thru-hiker's Planning Guide

Equipment Checklist

WEIGHT (in ounces)		ITEMS CARRIED IN BACKPACK (at beginning of hike)	DESCRIPTION OF ITEMS (make, model, size, etc.)
82		Backpack (empty) w/belt, accessories	JANSPORT BRYCE W/SB STRAPS
8		Raincover for backpack	JANSPORT (LARGE)
84		Tent (or tarp) w/accessories	MOSS STARLET (2-PERSON)
4		Plastic groundsheet to fit under tent (opt.)	60" X 84"
45		Sleeping bag w/stuff sack and garbage bag	CARIBOU PRIMALOFT 20°F
18		Sleeping pad w/nylon carrying sack	THERMAREST (3/4 LENGTH)
5		Groundcloth, nylon (opt.)	48" X 84"
1		Sitting pad (opt.)	
15	1/2	Stove (empty)	SVEA 123R W/O CUP
3	1/2	Fuel bottle (empty)	SIGG 16 OZ. W/ POUR SPOUT
12		Cookset (pots, pans, potholder, etc.)	1 QT. POT & LID, 1 PT. POT, SPOON, CUP,
—		~~Cooking utensils (excluding knife)~~	LIGHTER, SCOUR PAD, SSACK)
—		Butane lighter (or matches)	(IN COOKSET)
3		Water bottle(s), 1-pint (wide-mouth)	NALGENE LEXAN (1 EA.)
5		Water bottle(s), 1-quart (wide-mouth)	NALGENE LEXAN (1 EA.)
4		Water bag, 1-2 gallon carrying capacity	2 GAL. CAPACITY W/ SPOUT
5		Water purifier (chemical or filter type)	FILTER, TIMBERLINE (IN ZIPLOC)
9		First-aid kit (from Kits Checklist)	
7		Grooming kit (from Kits Checklist)	
4		Toilet kit (from Kits Checklist)	
4		Misc./repair kit (from Kits Checklist)	
1		Sewing kit (from Kits Checklist)	
3	1/2	Knife	SWISS ARMY SPARTAN
4		Flashlight w/batteries	MAGLITE W/AA BATTERIES
0	1/2	Candle lantern and/or candle (opt.)	CANDLE
1		Compass	SILVA TYPE A
—		Whistle	(INCL. IN MISC./REPAIR KIT)
3		Cord (1/8" diameter x 50' in length)	
10		Camera w/batteries (opt.)	OLYMPUS INFINITY W/ BATTERY
3		Camera kit (from Kits Checklist)	
3		Radio ~~or cassette player~~ (opt.)	SONY SPORTS WALKMAN W/BATTERIES
16		Datapouch (guidebooks, journal, pen, etc.)	
122		Clothing (from Clothing Checklist)	
13		Fuel (1 fluid oz. = 0.8 oz. weight)	16 OZ. COLEMAN FUEL
16		Water (1 pint = 16 oz. weight)	16 OZ.
2		FLOWER FINDER	NATURE STUDY GUILD
None		Hiking stick (hand carried, no pack weight)	TRACKS 3-SECTION
517 ozs.		TOTAL ESTIMATED PACK WEIGHT (without food) = (__32__ lbs. __5__ ozs.)	

Sample Planning Notebook

Kits Checklist

✓	First-aid Kit Weight: _9_ ounces
✓	Aspirin (or equivalent) 20 EA.
✓	Antibiotic ointment
	Skin cream or Vaseline, small tube (opt.)
	Cortisone cream (opt.)
✓	Eyedrops (Visine or equivalent)
	Toothache medicine (opt.)
✓	Athlete's foot medicine
✓	Powder (for chafing)
✓	Antacid tablets Tums
✓	Lip balm (Chapstick or Blistex)
	Diarrhea medicine (opt.)
	Allergy medicine (opt.)
✓	Bandaids (a few for minor cuts) 3 EA.
✓	Gauze, 1"-wide roll
✓	Sterile pads, 2"x2" (a few for larger cuts) 3 EA.
✓	Sterile pad, large (a few for bigger wounds) 1 EA.
✓	Adhesive tape (or surgical tape)
✓	Ace bandage (2"-wide)
✓	Moleskin or equivalent (2 PKGS. TO START)
✓	Second Skin by Spenco (opt.) (½ PKG.)
✓	Scissors, manicure type (opt.)
	Tweezers (opt.)
	Snakebite kit (opt.)

NOTE: CORTISONE CREAM IN DAMASCUS MD, AVON SKIN-SO-SOFT IN DAMASCUS MD

✓	Grooming Kit Weight: _7_ ounces
✓	Toothbrush
✓	Toothpaste
✓	Dental floss
✓	Biodegradeable soap (1 OZ. BOTTLE)
✓	Deodorant (opt.)
✓	Comb (opt.)
	Hair brush (opt.)
✓	Nail clippers
✓	Razor (opt.)
	Mirror (opt.)
	Washcloth (opt.)
	Towel (opt.)
✓	BAKING SODA (FOR TEETH)

✓	Toilet Kit Weight: _4_ ounces
✓	Toilet paper (in Ziploc bag)
	Tampons/sanitary napkins
✓	Matches
	Trowel (opt.)

✓	Miscellaneous/repair Kit Weight: _4_ ounces
✓	Spare parts for backpack
✓	Therm-A-Rest repair kit
✓	Extra flashlight bulb(s)
	Stove repair kit
✓	Extra batteries (AAA) (AA) (C) (9v)
✓	Boot glue
✓	Boot waterproofing

NOTE: AA FOR FLASHLIGHT AAA FOR RADIO

✓	Sewing Kit Weight: _1_ ounces
✓	Needles
✓	Top-stitching thread (black)
✓	Regular thread (wrapped around paper)
✓	Thimble, plastic
✓	Buttons (a few to match clothing)
✓	Safety pins (a few, assorted sizes)

✓	Camera Kit Weight: _3_ ounces
✓	Lens paper
	Lens cleaning solution (opt.)
✓	Lens blower-brush
✓	Tabletop tripod (opt.) ULTRAPOD
✓	Film, ASA# (100) (200) (400) 36 SLIDES
	Film, ASA# (100) (200) (400)
	Film, ASA# (100) (200) (400)

The Thru-hiker's Planning Guide

Clothing and Footwear Checklist

WEIGHT (in ounces)		CLOTHING ITEMS CARRIED IN BACKPACK (at beginning of hike)	Qty.	DESCRIPTION OF ITEMS (brand, size, color, etc.)
		Hiking footwear:		
18		Hiking socks	5 PR.	THORLO KX-11
		Sock liners		
		Warm-weather clothing:		
7		Hiking shorts	3 PR.	NYLON SOCCER w/ POLYPRO BRIEF
2		Underpants/~~bra~~ (opt.)	1 PR.	COTTON, BRIEFS
11		Hiking shirts, short-sleeve	3 PR.	NYLON SOCCER (LIGHTWEIGHT)
5		Hiking shirts, long-sleeve	1 PR.	NYLON SOCCER
10		Pants, long (opt.)	2 PR.	MULTISPORT TIGHTS, LYCRA
10		Sweater, lightweight (or equivalent garment)	1 EA.	WOOL
16		Jacket, lightweight (or equivalent garment)	1 EA.	POLARTEC 300
		Cold-weather clothing:		
		Underpants, thermal		
		Undershirts, thermal		
		Sweater, heavy (or equivalent garment)		
		Parka, lined (or equivalent garment)		
2		Ski cap, wool (or equivalent garment)	1 EA.	WOOL (RED)
1		Gloves	1 PR.	POLYPRO LINERS
		Rainwear:		
		Rainpants		
16		Rain jacket	1 EA.	MARMOT GORETEX w/ PIT ZIPS
		Poncho		
		Gaiters		
		Town clothes:		
12		~~Sneakers or~~ sandals	1 PR.	TEVA (OPEN TOE)
3		Town socks (opt.)	2 PR.	THORLO G-11 ROLLTOPS
		Town shirt (opt.)		
2		Town pants (opt.)	1 PR.	NYLON RUNNING SHORTS
		Accessories:		
2	½	Wallet	1 EA.	NYLON
2	½	Clothes bag w/plastic bag liner	1 EA.	
2		BANDANNA	1 EA.	EXTRA (FOR USE AS TOWEL)
122 ozs.		**TOTAL ESTIMATED CLOTHING WEIGHT (in pack)** = (__7__ lbs. __10__ ozs.)		

Sample Planning Notebook

Clothing and Footwear Checklist
(page 2)

ITEMS WORN TO START HIKE (assuming warm weather)	Qty.	DESCRIPTION OF ITEMS: (brand, size, color, etc.)
Hiking boots	1 pr.	Vasque Skywalk
Hiking socks	1 pr.	Thorlo KX-11
Sock liners (opt.)		
Hiking shirt, short sleeve	1 ea.	Nylon Soccer (lightweight)
Hiking shorts	1 ea.	Nylon Soccer w/ Polypro brief
Hat or cap (opt.)	1 ea.	Cotton, crushable
Bandana	1 ea.	Large
Wristwatch (opt.)	1 ea.	Casio Sports Altimeter

Note: Do not include the weight of the above items in the clothing weight recorded on your Equipment Checklist, since these items will not be carried in your pack. However, do not forget to include them when calculating quantities of clothing to purchase for your trip.

Clothing and footwear items to be packed in maildrops:

MD#	Maildrop Location	Clothing and Footwear Items
5	Damascus, VA	Nylon Soccer Shorts (2 pr.)
		Mesh Soccer Jerseys (3 pr.)
10	Harpers Ferry, WV	Socks, Thorlo KX-11 (5 pr.)
		Boots, Merrell Wilderness
19	Glencliff, NH	Sweater, wool lightweight (1 ea.)
		Rainpants, GoreTex (1 ea.)
		Gloves, Polypro liners (1 pr.)
		Underwear, Thermax lightweight (1 pr.)

Note: Northbounders should pick up extra cold-weather items for going through the White Mountains at Hanover or Glencliff, New Hampshire. Southbounders usually pick up cold-weather items no later than Damascus, Virginia, and, depending on the year, may need them earlier.

Menu Planner

Meal #	Breakfast	Lunch	Supper	Snacks
1	Pop Tarts (2/pkgs) Milk (½ qt.) Coffee	Kudos (2 bars) Kool-Aid (1 pt.)	Kraft 3-season Herb Tuna (small can) Margarine Milk (½ qt.) Tea M & Ms	Apple Cider Mix Hot Cocoa Mix Dried Fruit Mix Sunflower Seeds Snickers Bars
2	Granola Mix (4 oz.) Milk (½ qt.) Coffee	Gorp (4 oz.) Kool-Aid (1 pt.)	Lipton Pasta Alfredo Tuna (small can) Margarine Milk (½ qt.) Tea M & Ms	Buy more on the trail
3	Pancake Mix (4 oz.) Milk (½ qt.)	Trail Mix (4 oz.) Kool-Aid (1 pt.)	Lipton Pasta S. Cr. Tuna (small can) Margarine Milk (½ qt.) Tea M & Ms	
4	Buy more on the trail	Buy more on the trail	Lipton Pasta Parm. Tuna (small can) Margarine Milk (½ qt.) Tea M & Ms	
5			Mac & Cheese Tuna (small can) Margarine Milk (½ qt.) Tea M & M's	

Sample Planning Notebook

Food List

Meal	Food Item	Servings Needed	Amount per Serving	Total Amount	Unit Price	Total Cost
B R E A K F A S T	Pop Tarts (2/pkg.)	55	1 pkg.	55 pkgs.	.25/pkg.	13.75
	Granola Mix	73	4 oz.	19 lbs.	1.35/lb.	25.65
	Pancake Mix	4	4 oz.	1 box	1.56/box	1.56
	Powdered Milk	264*	½ pkg.	132 pkgs.	.38/pkg.	50.16
	Coffee, Instant	132	1 pkg.	132 pkgs.	.21/pkg.	27.72
	132 Breakfasts					
L U N C H	Kudos Bars	30	2 bars	60 bars	.13/bar	7.80
	GORP { Raisins, Golden	56	~1 oz.	4 lbs.	1.59/lb.	6.36
	Peanuts, Roasted	56	~2 oz.	7 lbs.	1.19/lb.	8.33
	Tollhouse Morsels	56	~1 oz.	3 lbs.	2.19/lb.	6.57
	Trail Mix	50	4 oz.	12 lbs.	1.29/lb.	15.48
	Kool-Aid w/Sugar 134 Lunches	134	¼ pkg.	37 pkgs.	.59/pkg.	21.83
S U P P E R	Kraft 3-Season Herb	22	1 pkg.	22 pkgs.	1.00/pkg.	22.00
	Lipton Pasta Alfredo	23	1 pkg.	23 pkgs.	1.00/pkg.	23.00
	Lipton Pasta Sour Cr.	22	1 pkg.	22 pkgs.	1.00/pkg.	22.00
	Lipton Pasta Parmesan	42	1 pkg.	42 pkgs.	1.00/pkg.	42.00
	Mac & Cheese Dinner	22	1 pkg.	22 pkgs.	1.00/pkg.	22.00
	Tuna in Oil (small can)	131	3 oz. can	131 cans	.34/can	44.54
	Powdered Milk	131	½ pkg.	(included w/breakfasts)		
	Tea	258	1 bag	258 bags	.05/bag	12.90
	M&Ms (small pkg.)	131	1 pkg.	131 pkgs.	.14/pkg.	18.34
	131 Suppers					
S N A C K S	Apple Cider Mix	44	1 pkg.	44 pkgs.	.24/pkg.	10.56
	Hot Cocoa Mix	28	1 pkg.	28 pkgs.	.22/pkg.	6.16
	Dried Fruit Mix	26	3 oz.	5 lbs.	1.90/lb.	9.50
	Sunflower Seeds	16	2 oz. pkg.	16 pkgs.	.49/pkg.	7.84
	Snickers Bars (bite size, 26/bag)	199	several	8 bags	1.96/bag	15.68
	Vitamins (Centrum)	182	1/day	182	.06/ea.	10.92
					Total Estimated Cost	$452.65

The Thru-hiker's Planning Guide

Supplies and Misc. Items Lists

Supplies	Used on the Trail for:	Number Needed	Unit Price	Total Cost
Toilet Paper, unscented (24 x ½ roll)		12 rolls	.26/roll	3.12
Toothpaste, sample size		12 tubes	.49/tube	5.88
Dental Floss		6 pkgs.	1.14/pkg.	6.84
Garbage Bags	Protect SB, Clothes	2 boxes	1.79/box	3.58
Large Ziploc Bags	Garbage	2 boxes	1.49/box	2.98
Small Ziploc Bags	Repacking Food	3 boxes	1.49/box	4.47
Razors, Disposable		1 doz.	.25/ea.	3.00
Baking Soda	Cleaning Teeth	1 box	.79/box	.79
Moleskin		5 pkgs.	2.19/pkg.	10.95
Detergent, Unscented	Laundry in Towns	1 lg. box	3.59/box	3.59
			Total Estimated Cost	$45.20

Misc. Items	Used on the Trail for:	Number Needed	Unit Price	Total Cost
Film, ASA 200 - 36 slides		31 rolls	3.57/roll	110.67
Batteries, AA	Flashlight	18 ea.	.25 ea.	4.50
Batteries, AAA	Radio	26 ea.	.26 ea.	6.76
Butane Lighters		6 ea.	.79 ea.	4.74
Cortisone Cream	Bites, Poison Ivy	1 tube	4.58 ea.	4.58
Aspirin		100 ea.	1.98/c	1.98
Notebook, Spiral	Journal	5 ea.	1.09 ea.	5.45
Avon Skin-So-Soft (1 oz.)	No-see-ums	1 ea.	1.99 ea.	1.99
			Total Estimated Cost	$136.09

Sample Planning Notebook

Hiking Schedule
(page 1)

Day #	Date	Day	Miles	Destination	MD#	B	L	S
				START HIKE AT AMICALOLA FALLS STATE PARK, GEORGIA —				
001	4/4	W	8.9	SPRINGER MTN. SHELTER		–	X	X
002	4/5	TH	7.4	HAWK MTN. SHELTER		X	X	X
003	4/6	F	8.5	GOOCH GAP SHELTER		X	X	X
004	4/7	S	12.3	BLOOD MTN. SHELTER (NO WATER)		X	X	X
005	4/8	SN	2.3	NEELS GAP, WALASIYI CTR., BUNKROOM	BUY	X	G	G
006	4/9	M	10.6	LOW GAP SHELTER		G	G	G
007	4/10	TU	8.0	BLUE MTN. SHELTER		G	G	G
008	4/11	W	12.2	ADDIS GAP SHELTER		G	G	G
009	4/12	TH	9.7	PLUMORCHARD GAP SHELTER		G	G	G
010	4/13	F	12.3	STANDING INDIAN SHELTER		G	G	G
011	4/14	S	15.0	BIG SPRING SHELTER		G	G	G
012	4/15	SN	12.9	SILER BALD SHELTER (SIDE TRIP		G	–	–
—	—	—	—	TO RAINBOW SPRINGS CG FOR FOOD)	BUY	–	G	G
013	4/16	M	12.4	COLD SPRING SHELTER		G	G	G
014	4/17	TU	11.6	WESSER, NC; NOC BUNKROOM	①	G	G	R
015	4/18	W	7.8	CAMPSITE ON CHEOAH BALD		R	X	X
016	4/19	TH	13.1	CABLE GAP SHELTER (SIDE TRIP		X	X	X
—	—	—	—	TO FONTANA DAM, NC FOR FOOD)	②	X	X	–
017	4/20	F	7.0	FONTANA DAM SHELTER		–	–	R
018	4/21	S	6.1	GSMNP – BIRCH SPRING SHELTER		X	X	X
019	4/22	SN	9.2	GSMNP – SPENCE FIELD SHELTER		X	X	X
020	4/23	M	11.4	GSMNP – SILERS BALD SHELTER		X	X	X
021	4/24	TU	7.6	GSMNP – MT. COLLINS SHELTER		X	X	X
022	4/25	W	7.3	GSMNP – ICEWATER SPRING SHELTER		X	–	–
—	—	—	—	(SIDE TRIP TO GATLINBURG, TN FOR FOOD)	BUY	–	G	G
023	4/26	TH	7.4	GSMNP – PECKS CORNER SHELTER		G	G	G
024	4/27	F	12.0	GSMNP – COSBY KNOB SHELTER		G	G	G
025	4/28	S	17.5	GROUNDHOG CREEK SHELTER		G	G	G
026	4/29	SN	11.3	ROARING FORK SHELTER		G	G	G
027	4/30	M	10.3	DEER PARK MTN. SHELTER		G	G	G
028	5/1	TU	3.2	HOT SPRINGS, NC, JESUIT HOSTEL	③	G	R	R
029	5/2	W	NONE	" " " " "		R	R	R

Key to symbols and abbreviations: **MD**=maildrop, **B**=breakfast, **L**=lunch, **S**=supper, **X**=meal from maildrop, **G**=meal from grocery store, **R**=meal from restaurant, **A**=meal included in price of lodging (American plan)

The Thru-hiker's Planning Guide

Hiking Schedule
(page 2)

Day #	Date	Day	Miles	Destination	MD#	B	L	S
030	5/3	TH	10.9	SPRING MTN. SHELTER		R	X	X
031	5/4	F	15.3	JERRY CABIN SHELTER		X	X	X
032	5/5	S	14.2	HOGBACK RIDGE SHELTER		X	X	X
033	5/6	SN	9.2	BALD MTN. SHELTER		X	X	X
034	5/7	M	9.6	NO BUSINESS KNOB SHELTER		X	X	X
035	5/8	TU	10.8	NOLICHUCKY RETREAT CG (SIDE TRIP		X	—	—
—	—	—	—	TO ERWIN, TN FOR MD)	④	—	R	R
036	5/9	W	2.9	CURLEY MAPLE GAP SHELTER		X	X	X
037	5/10	TH	12.2	CHERRY GAP SHELTER		X	X	X
038	5/11	F	14.1	ROAN HIGH KNOB SHELTER		X	X	X
039	5/12	S	13.7	APPLE HOUSE SHELTER		X	X	X
040	5/13	SN	14.1	MORELAND GAP SHELTER		X	X	X
041	5/14	M	7.2	LAUREL FORK SHELTER		X	X	X
042	5/15	TU	10.5	WATAUGA LAKE SHELTER		G	X	X
043	5/16	W	13.0	IRON MTN. SHELTER		X	X	X
044	5/17	TH	16.2	ABINGDON GAP SHELTER		X	X	X
045	5/18	F	9.8	DAMASCUS, VA, HOSTEL	⑤	X	R	R
046	5/19	S	NONE	" " "		R	R	R
047	5/20	SN	9.5	SAUNDERS SHELTER		R	R	X
048	5/21	M	16.9	DEEP GAP SHELTER		X	X	X
049	5/22	TU	13.0	OLD ORCHARD SHELTER		X	X	X
050	5/23	W	14.2	TRIMPI SHELTER		X	X	X
051	5/24	TH	21.9	ATKINS, VA, MOTEL		X	X	R
052	5/25	F	14.8	KNOT MOLE BRANCH SHELTER		R	X	X
053	5/26	S	19.9	JENKINS SHELTER		X	X	X
054	5/27	SN	11.6	BASTIAN, VA, HOSTEL (MD @ LEVI'S)	⑥	X	R	R
055	5/28	M	12.1	JENNY KNOB SHELTER		R	X	X
056	5/29	TU	19.5	WOODSHOLE		X	X	X
057	5/30	W	10.5	PEARISBURG, VA, HOSTEL	⑦	X	R	R
058	5/31	TH	18.2	PINE SWAMP BRANCH SHELTER		R	X	X
059	6/1	F	11.9	WAR SPUR SHELTER		X	X	X
060	6/2	S	18.5	NIDAY SHELTER		X	X	X
061	6/3	SN	22.3	CATAWBA MTN. SHELTER		X	X	X

Key to symbols and abbreviations: **MD**=maildrop, **B**=breakfast, **L**=lunch, **S**=supper, **X**=meal from maildrop, **G**=meal from grocery store, **R**=meal from restaurant, **A**=meal included in price of lodging (American plan)

Sample Planning Notebook

Hiking Schedule
(page 3)

Day #	Date	Day	Miles	Destination	MD#	B	L	S
062	6/4	M	8.2	LAMBERTS MEADOW SHELTER		X	X	X
063	6/5	TU	11.5	TROUTVILLE, VA, MOTEL	⑧	X	R	R
064	6/6	W	9.9	WILSON CREEK SHELTER		R	X	X
065	6/7	TH	12.9	COVE MTN. SHELTER (NO WATER)		X	X	X
066	6/8	F	15.9	THUNDER HILL SHELTER		X	X	X
067	6/9	S	12.4	MATTS CREEK SHELTER		X	X	X
068	6/10	SN	13.6	PUNCHBOWL SHELTER		X	X	X
069	6/11	M	8.8	BROWN MTN. CREEK SHELTER		X	X	X
070	6/12	TU	15.0	SEELEY-WOODSWORTH SHELTER		X	X	X
071	6/13	W	14.2	HARPERS CREEK SHELTER		X	X	X
072	6/14	TH	6.2	RUSTY'S HARD TIME HOLLOW		X	X	X
073	6/15	F	18.4	WAYNESBORO, VA, FIRE STATION	⑨	X	X	R
074	6/16	S	NONE	" " "		R	R	R
075	6/17	SN	6.9	CALF MTN. SHELTER		R	R	X
076	6/18	M	13.2	SNP - BLACKROCK HUT		X	X	X
077	6/19	TU	13.1	SNP - PINEFIELD HUT		X	X	X
078	6/20	W	8.3	SNP - HIGH TOP HUT		X	X	X
079	6/21	TH	12.5	SNP - BEARFENCE MTN. HUT		X	X	X
080	6/22	F	11.4	SNP - ROCK SPRING HUT		X	X	X
081	6/23	S	15.0	SNP - PASS MTN. HUT		X	X	X
082	6/24	SN	23.1	TOM FLOYD WAYSIDE		X	X	X
083	6/25	M	13.9	MANASSAS GAP SHELTER		X	X	X
084	6/26	TU	13.6	ROD HOLLOW SHELTER		X	X	X
085	6/27	W	17.5	BLACKBURN A.T. CENTER		X	X	X
086	6/28	TH	11.8	HARPERS FERRY, WV, HOTEL	⑩	X	R	R
087	6/29	F	16.2	ROCKY RUN SHELTER		R	X	X
088	6/30	S	23.6	PEN MAR COUNTY PARK, PAVILION		X	X	X
089	7/1	SN	19.9	QUARRY GAP SHELTERS		X	X	X
090	7/2	M	17.4	PINE GROVE FURNACE ST. PK., HOSTEL		X	X	X
091	7/3	TU	7.3	TAGG RUN SHELTERS		X	X	X
092	7/4	W	11.9	BOILING SPRINGS, PA, CAMPSITE		X	X	R
093	7/5	TH	15.5	DARLINGTON SHELTER		X	X	X
094	7/6	F	11.4	DUNCANNON, PA, HOTEL	⑪	X	R	R

Key to symbols and abbreviations: **MD**=maildrop, **B**=breakfast, **L**=lunch, **S**=supper, **X**=meal from maildrop, **G**=meal from grocery store, **R**=meal from restaurant, **A**=meal included in price of lodging (American plan)

The Thru-hiker's Planning Guide

Hiking Schedule
(page 4)

Day #	Date	Day	Miles	Destination	MD#	B	L	S
095	7/7	S	NONE	" " "		R	R	R
096	7/8	SN	12.3	PETERS MTN. SHELTER		R	X	X
097	7/9	M	17.0	RAUSCH GAP SHELTER		X	X	X
098	7/10	TU	16.7	PA 501, BMEHC SHELTER		X	X	X
099	7/11	W	21.9	PORT CLINTON, PA, PAVILION	(12)	X	X	X
100	7/12	TH	6.3	WINDSOR FURNACE SHELTER		R	X	X
101	7/13	F	18.1	ALLENTOWN HIKING CLUB SHELTER		X	X	X
102	7/14	S	10.9	BAKE OVEN KNOB SHELTER		X	R	X
103	7/15	SN	12.2	CAMPSITE AT SPRING		X	X	X
104	7/16	M	12.3	LEROY SMITH SHELTER		X	X	X
105	7/17	TU	19.8	DELAWARE WATER GAP, PA, HOSTEL	(13)	X	X	R
106	7/18	W	NONE	" " " " "		R	R	R
107	7/19	TH	7.2	CAMPSITE ON KITTATINNY MTN.		R	X	X
108	7/20	F	17.5	BRINK RD. SHELTER		X	X	X
109	7/21	S	19.7	HIGH POINT SHELTER		X	X	X
110	7/22	SN	19.3	VERNON, NJ, FIRE PAVILION		X	X	R
111	7/23	M	17.5	CAMPSITE AT WATER PUMP		X	X	X
112	7/24	TU	16.4	FINGERBOARD SHELTER (NO WATER)		X	X	X
113	7/25	W	8.5	WEST MTN. SHELTER (NO WATER)		X	X	X
114	7/26	TH	11.6	GRAYMOOR FRIARY (SIDE TRIP		X	—	—
—	—	—	—	TO BEAR MTN. P.O. FOR MD)	(14)	—	R	A
115	7/27	F	19.4	RPH CABIN		A	X	X
116	7/28	S	16.1	TELEPHONE PIONEERS SHELTER		X	X	X
117	7/29	SN	13.0	CAMPSITE AT TEN MILE RIVER		X	X	X
118	7/30	M	15.6	STEWART HOLLOW BROOK SHELTER		X	—	—
—	—	—	—	(SIDE TRIP TO KENT, CT FOR MD)	(15)	—	R	X
119	7/31	TU	20.7	LIMESTONE SPRING SHELTER		X	X	X
120	8/1	W	12.7	CAMPSITE AT BEAR ROCK FALLS		X	X	X
121	8/2	TH	18.0	TOM LEONARD SHELTER		X	X	X
122	8/3	F	19.8	UPPER GOOSE POND CABIN (FEE)		X	X	X
123	8/4	S	NONE	" " " "		X	X	X
124	8/5	SN	17.6	KAY WOOD SHELTER		X	X	X
125	8/6	M	11.2	CHESHIRE, MA, CHURCH	(16)	X	R	R

Key to symbols and abbreviations: **MD**=maildrop, **B**=breakfast, **L**=lunch, **S**=supper, **X**=meal from maildrop, **G**=meal from grocery store, **R**=meal from restaurant, **A**=meal included in price of lodging (American plan)

Sample Planning Notebook

Hiking Schedule
(page 5)

Day #	Date	Day	Miles	Destination	MD#	B	L	S
126	8/7	Tu	11.6	Wilbur Clearing Leanto		R	X	X
127	8/8	W	16.9	Congdon Camp Shelter		X	X	X
128	8/9	Th	14.0	Goddard Shelter		X	X	X
129	8/10	F	18.5	Stratton Pond Shelter		X	X	X
130	8/11	S	10.3	Manchester Center, VT, Church	(17)	X	R	R
131	8/12	Sn	None	" " " "		R	R	R
132	8/13	M	3.6	Mad Tom Shelter		R	X	X
133	8/14	Tu	12.4	Big Branch Shelter		X	X	X
134	8/15	W	8.5	Greenwall Shelter		X	X	X
135	8/16	Th	14.0	Gov. Clement Shelter		X	X	X
136	8/17	F	12.2	Kent Pond, B & B		X	X	X
137	8/18	S	15.1	Wintturi Shelter		A	X	X
138	8/19	Sn	21.3	Happy Hill Cabin		X	X	X
139	8/20	M	5.9	Hanover, NH, Frat House	(18)	X	R	R
140	8/21	Tu	None	" " " "		R	R	R
141	8/22	W	17.8	Trapper John Shelter		R	X	X
142	8/23	Th	18.1	Atwell Rd., DOC Cabin		X	X	X
143	8/24	F	9.1	Jeffers Brook Shelter (side trip		X	X	X
—	—	—	—	to Glencliff, NH for MD)	(19)	—	—	—
144	8/25	S	14.7	Eliza Brook Shelter		X	X	X
145	8/26	Sn	11.1	Liberty Spring Campsite (fee)		X	X	X
146	8/27	M	7.6	Garfield Ridge Shelter (fee)		X	X	X
147	8/28	Tu	13.7	Ethan Pond Shelter (fee)		X	X	X
148	8/29	W	14.0	Lakes of the Clouds Hut (fee)		X	X	X
149	8/30	Th	10.1	Osgood Tentsite		X	X	X
150	8/31	F	9.8	Carter Notch AMC Hut (fee)		X	X	A
151	9/1	S	12.9	Rattle River Shelter		A	X	X
152	9/2	Sn	1.6	Gorham, NH (MD to hostel)	(20)	X	R	R
153	9/3	M	None	" "		R	R	R
154	9/4	Tu	11.9	Gentian Pond Shelter		R	X	X
155	9/5	W	9.3	Full Goose Shelter		X	X	X
156	9/6	Th	5.1	Speck Pond Shelter (fee)		X	X	X
157	9/7	F	10.4	Frye Notch Leanto		X	X	X

Key to symbols and abbreviations: **MD**=maildrop, **B**=breakfast, **L**=lunch, **S**=supper, **X**=meal from maildrop, **G**=meal from grocery store, **R**=meal from restaurant, **A**=meal included in price of lodging (American plan)

Hiking Schedule

(page 6)

Day #	Date	Day	Miles	Destination	MD#	B	L	S
158	9/8	S	4.6	ANDOVER, ME, HOSTEL	(21)	X	R	R
159	9/9	SN	6.1	HALL MTN. LEANTO		R	X	X
160	9/10	M	12.1	BEMIS MTN. LEANTO		X	X	X
161	9/11	TU	13.1	SABBATH DAY POND LEANTO		X	X	X
162	9/12	W	10.6	PIAZZA ROCK LEANTO		X	X	X
163	9/13	TH	16.3	SPAULDING MTN. LEANTO		X	X	X
164	9/14	F	12.6	STRATTON, ME, HOTEL	(22)	X	X	R
165	9/15	S	5.3	HORNS POND LEANTO		R	R	X
166	9/16	SN	9.7	LITTLE BIGELOW LEANTO		X	X	X
167	9/17	M	16.9	PIERCE POND LEANTO		X	X	X
—	—	—	—	KENNEBEC RIVER CROSSING		—	—	—
168	9/18	TU	9.6	PLEASANT POND LEANTO		X	G	G
169	9/19	W	12.3	MOXIE BALD MTN. LEANTO		X	X	X
170	9/20	TH	18.0	MONSON, ME, SHAW'S BOARDING HOME	(23)	X	X	A
171	9/21	F	NONE	" " " " "		A	R	A
172	9/22	S	3.1	LEEMAN BROOK LEANTO		A	R	X
173	9/23	SN	16.2	CLOUD POND LEANTO		X	X	X
174	9/24	M	6.8	CHAIRBACK GAP LEANTO		X	X	X
175	9/25	TU	9.6	CARL NEWHALL LEANTO		X	X	X
176	9/26	W	6.7	LOGAN BROOK LEANTO		X	X	X
177	9/27	TH	11.6	COOPER BROOK FALLS LEANTO		X	X	X
178	9/28	F	11.1	POTAYWADJO SPRING LEANTO		X	X	X
179	9/29	S	17.9	RAINBOW STREAM LEANTO		X	X	X
180	9/30	SN	14.6	ABOL BRIDGE STORE, CAMPSITE	BUY	X	X	G
181	10/1	M	7.3	DAICEY POND LEANTOS		G	G	G
182	10/2	TU	7.2	BAXTER PEAK, KATAHDIN		G	G	—

Key to symbols and abbreviations: **MD**=maildrop, **B**=breakfast, **L**=lunch, **S**=supper, **X**=meal from maildrop, **G**=meal from grocery store, **R**=meal from restaurant, **A**=meal included in price of lodging (American plan)

Maildrop Packing List

Breakfast

MD#	Maildrop Location	Number of breakfasts needed in each maildrop	Pop Tarts (2/pkg.)	Granola Mix (4 oz.)	Pancake Mix (4 oz.)	Powdered Milk (½ pkg.)	Coffee, Instant (1 serv)	Vitamins (1/day)					
0	START OF HIKE	4		4		4	4	14					
1	WESSER, NC	2	1	1		2	2	4					
2	FONTANA DAM, NC	5	2	2	1	5	5	6					
3	HOT SPRINGS, NC	5	2	3		5	5	7					
4	ERWIN, TN	9	4	5		9	9	10					
5	DAMASCUS, VA	6	3	3		6	6	8					
6	BASTIAN, VA	2	1	1		2	2	4					
7	PEARISBURG, VA	5	2	3		5	5	7					
8	TROUTVILLE, VA	9	4	5		9	9	10					
9	WAYNESBORO, VA	11	5	5	1	11	11	12					
10	HARPERS FERRY, WV	7	3	4		7	7	9					
11	DUNCANNON, PA	3	1	2		3	3	5					
12	PORT CLINTON, PA	5	2	3		5	5	7					
13	DELAWARE WATER GAP, PA	7	3	4		7	7	8					
14	BEAR MOUNTAIN, NY	3	1	2		3	3	5					
15	KENT, CT	7	3	4		7	7	9					
16	CHESHIRE, MA	4	2	2		4	4	6					
17	MANCHESTER CTR., VT	6	2	3	1	6	6	8					
18	HANOVER, NH	2	1	1		2	2	4					
19	GLENCLIFF, NH	8	4	4		8	8	9					
20	GORHAM, NH	4	2	2		4	4	6					
21	ANDOVER, ME	5	2	3		5	5	7					
22	STRATTON, ME	5	2	3		5	5	7					
23	MONSON, ME	8	3	4	1	8	8	10					
	Totals	132	55	73	x	132	132	182					

The Thru-hiker's Planning Guide

Maildrop Packing List

		Lunch items to be packed in maildrop:									
Lunch	Number of lunches needed in each maildrop	Kudos (2 bars)	Gorp (4 oz.)	Trail Mix (4 oz.)	Kool-Aid (1 pkg/4 days)						
MD# / Maildrop Location											
0 START OF HIKE	4		4		1						
1 WESSER, NC	3	1	1	1	1						
2 FONTANA DAM, NC	4	1	2	1	1						
3 HOT SPRINGS, NC	5	2	2	1	1						
4 ERWIN, TN	9	3	3	3	2						
5 DAMASCUS, VA	6	2	2	2	2						
6 BASTIAN, VA	2	1	1		1						
7 PEARISBURG, VA	5	1	2	2	1						
8 TROUTVILLE, VA	10	3	4	3	3						
9 WAYNESBORO, VA	10	3	4	3	3						
10 HARPERS FERRY, WV	7	2	3	2	2						
11 DUNCANNON, PA	4	1	2	1	1						
12 PORT CLINTON, PA	5	2	2	1	1						
13 DELAWARE WATER GAP, PA	7	3	3	1	2						
14 BEAR MOUNTAIN, NY	3	1	1	1	1						
15 KENT, CT	6	2	2	2	2						
16 CHESHIRE, MA	4	1	2	1	1						
17 MANCHESTER CTR, VT	7	2	3	2	2						
18 HANOVER, NH	3	1	1	1	1						
19 GLENCLIFF, NH	8	3	3	2	2						
20 GORHAM, NH	4	1	2	1	1						
21 ANDOVER, ME	6	2	2	2	2						
22 STRATTON, ME	4	1	2	1	1						
23 MONSON, ME	8	3	3	2	2						
Totals	134	42	56	36	37						

Sample Planning Notebook

Maildrop Packing List

			|Supper items to be packed in maildrop:|								
MD#	Maildrop Location	Number of suppers needed in each maildrop	Kraft 3-season Herb	Lipton Pasta Alfredo	Lipton Pasta Sour Cr.	Lipton Pasta Parmesan	Mac & Cheese Dinner	Tuna in oil (3 oz. can)	Powdered Milk (½ pkg.)	Tea (1 bag/serv.)	M&Ms (small pkg.)	
0	START OF HIKE	4				2	2	4		4	4	
1	WESSER, NC	3	1	1	1			3		6	3	
2	FONTANA DAM, NC	4	1			2	1	4		8	4	
3	HOT SPRINGS, NC	5		1	1	2	1	5		10	5	
4	ERWIN, TN	9	2	2	2	2	1	9		18	9	
5	DAMASCUS, VA	6	1	1	1	2	1	6		12	6	
6	BASTIAN, VA	2	1	1				2	(INCLUDED IN BREAKFAST TOTALS)	4	2	
7	PEARISBURG, VA	5	1		1	2	1	5		10	5	
8	TROUTVILLE, VA	9	1	2	2	3	1	9		18	9	
9	WAYNESBORO, VA	11	2	2	2	3	2	11		22	11	
10	HARPERS FERRY, WV	6	1	1	1	2	1	6		12	6	
11	DUNCANNON, PA	4		1	1	2		4		8	4	
12	PORT CLINTON, PA	5	1	1	1	1	1	5		10	5	
13	DELAWARE WATER GAP, PA	6	1	1	1	2	1	6		12	6	
14	BEAR MOUNTAIN, NY	4	1	1		1	1	4		8	4	
15	KENT, CT	6	1	1	1	2	1	6		12	6	
16	CHESHIRE, MA	4			1	2	1	4		8	4	
17	MANCHESTER CTR., VT	7	2	1	1	2	1	7		14	7	
18	HANOVER, NH	3		1	1	1		3		6	3	
19	GLENCLIFF, NH	7	1	1	1	3	1	7		14	7	
20	GORHAM, NH	4	1	1	1		1	4		8	4	
21	ANDOVER, ME	5	1	1		2	1	5		10	5	
22	STRATTON, ME	4			1	2	1	4		8	4	
23	MONSON, ME	8	2	2	1	2	1	8		16	8	
	Totals	131	22	23	22	42	22	131	1	258	131	

The Thru-hiker's Planning Guide

Maildrop Packing List

Other foods to be packed in maildrop:

MD#	Maildrop Location	Apple Cider Mix	Hot Cocoa Mix	Dried Fruit Mix	Sunflower Seeds	Snickers Bars (bite size)							
0	START OF HIKE	2	2	1		8							
1	WESSER, NC	1	2	1		6							
2	FONTANA DAM, NC	1	2	1		8							
3	HOT SPRINGS, NC	2	3	1		10							
4	ERWIN, TN	3	5	1		12							
5	DAMASCUS, VA	2		1	1	12							
6	BASTIAN, VA	1		1	1	4							
7	PEARISBURG, VA	2		1	1	10							
8	TROUTVILLE, VA	3		2	2	12							
9	WAYNESBORO, VA	3		2	2	12							
10	HARPERS FERRY, WV	2		1	1	6							
11	DUNCANNON, PA	1		1	1	4							
12	PORT CLINTON, PA	2		1	1	5							
13	DELAWARE WATER GAP, PA	2		1	1	6							
14	BEAR MOUNTAIN, NY	1		1	1	4							
15	KENT, CT	2		1	1	6							
16	CHESHIRE, MA	1		1	1	4							
17	MANCHESTER CTR., VT	2		1	1	12							
18	HANOVER, NH	1		1	1	6							
19	GLENCLIFF, NH	2		1		12							
20	GORHAM, NH	1	3	1		8							
21	ANDOVER, ME	2	3	1		10							
22	STRATTON, ME	2	2	1		10							
23	MONSON, ME	3	6	1		12							
	Totals	44	28	26	16	199							

Sample Planning Notebook

Maildrop Packing List

	Supplies	Toilet Paper (½ roll)	Toothpaste (sample size)	Dental Floss	Garbage Bags	Large Ziploc Bags	Small Ziploc Bags	Razors (disposable)	Baking Soda (1 oz. pkg.)	Moleskin (pkg.)	Detergent (unscented)			
MD#	Maildrop Location													
0	START OF HIKE	1	1	1	1	1	2			2				
1	WESSER, NC	1			1	1	2	1	1	1	1			
2	FONTANA DAM, NC	1	1		1	1	2			1	1			
3	HOT SPRINGS, NC	1			1	1	2	1			1			
4	ERWIN, TN	1			1	1	2				1			
5	DAMASCUS, VA	1	1	1	2	1	4	1	1	1	1			
6	BASTIAN, VA	1			1	1	2							
7	PEARISBURG, VA	1	1		1	1	2	1	1		1			
8	TROUTVILLE, VA	1			1	1	2				1			
9	WAYNESBORO, VA	1	1	1	2	1	4	1	1					
10	HARPERS FERRY, WV	1			1	1	2				1			
11	DUNCANNON, PA	1	1		1	1	2	1	1		1			
12	PORT CLINTON, PA	1			1	1	2							
13	DELAWARE WATER GAP, PA	1	1	1	2	1	4	1	1		1			
14	BEAR MOUNTAIN, NY	1			1	1	2							
15	KENT, CT	1	1		1	1	2				1			
16	CHESHIRE, MA	1			1	1	2	1	1		1			
17	MANCHESTER CTR., VT	1	1	1	2	1	4	1			1			
18	HANOVER, NH	1			1	1	2	1	1		1			
19	GLENCLIFF, NH	1	1		2	1	2							
20	GORHAM, NH	1			1	1	2	1	1		1			
21	ANDOVER, ME	1	1	1	1	1	2							
22	STRATTON, ME	1			2	1	2				1			
23	MONSON, ME	1	1		2	1	8	1	1		1			
	Totals	24	12	6	31	24	62	12	10	5	18			

The Thru-hiker's Planning Guide

Maildrop Packing List

Misc. items to be packed in maildrop:

MD#	Maildrop Location	Guidebook Maps	Film, ASA 200 Slide	Batteries, AA	Batteries, AAA	Lighters, Butane	Cortisone Cream	Aspirin	Notebooks (Journal)	Avon Skin-So-Soft				
0	START OF HIKE	✓	2	2	2	1		20	1					
1	WESSER, NC		1		2									
2	FONTANA DAM, NC	✓	2	2										
3	HOT SPRINGS, NC	✓	1		2									
4	ERWIN, TN		1											
5	DAMASCUS, VA	✓	2	2	2	1	1	20	1	1				
6	BASTIAN, VA		1											
7	PEARISBURG, VA	✓	1		2									
8	TROUTVILLE, VA		1											
9	WAYNESBORO, VA	✓	2	2	2	1		20						
10	HARPERS FERRY, WV	✓	1						1					
11	DUNCANNON, PA		1	2	2									
12	PORT CLINTON, PA		1											
13	DELAWARE WATER GAP, PA	✓	1		2	1		20						
14	BEAR MOUNTAIN, NY	✓	1	2										
15	KENT, CT		1		2									
16	CHESHIRE, MA	✓	2						1					
17	MANCHESTER CTR., VT		1	2	2	1								
18	HANOVER, NH	✓	1					20						
19	GLENCLIFF, NH		2	2	2									
20	GORHAM, NH	✓	1											
21	ANDOVER, ME		1		2	1			1					
22	STRATTON, ME		1											
23	MONSON, ME	✓	2	2	2									
	Totals	OK	31	18	26	6	1	100	5	1				

Sample Planning Notebook

Maildrop Posting Schedule

MD#	Maildrop Location	ZIP Code	Due Date	Mailing Date
1	WESSER, NC (c/o NOC)	*	April 17	April 3
2	FONTANA DAM, NC	28733	April 20	April 3
3	HOT SPRINGS, NC	28743	May 1	April 13
4	ERWIN, TN	37650	May 8	April 13
5	DAMASCUS, VA	24236	May 18	April 27
6	BASTIAN, VA (c/o LEVI'S)	**	May 27	May 4
7	PEARISBURG, VA	24134	May 30	May 11
8	TROUTVILLE, VA	24175	June 5	May 18
9	WAYNESBORO, VA	22980	June 15	May 25
10	HARPERS FERRY, WV	25425	June 28	June 8
11	DUNCANNON, PA	17020	July 6	June 15
12	PORT CLINTON, PA	19549	July 11	June 15
13	DELAWARE WATER GAP, PA	18327	July 17	June 22
14	BEAR MOUNTAIN, NY	10911	July 26	July 6
15	KENT, CT	06757	July 30	July 13
16	CHESHIRE, MA	01225	August 6	July 13
17	MANCHESTER CTR., VT	05255	August 11	July 20
18	HANOVER, NH	03755	August 20	July 27
19	GLENCLIFF, NH	03238	August 24	August 3
20	GORHAM, NH (c/o GOR. HSE.)	***	September 2	August 10
21	ANDOVER, ME	04216	September 8	August 18
22	STRATTON, ME	04982	September 14	August 18
23	MONSON, ME	04464	September 20	August 31

* NANTAHALA OUTDOOR CENTER, BOX 41, US 19W, BRYSON CITY, NC 28713
** LEVI LONG, P.O. BOX 42, BASTIAN, VA 24314
*** GORHAM HOUSE INN, 55 MAIN ST., GORHAM, NH 03581

Mailing Instructions:

All packages sent to post offices should be addressed as follows:

Your Name
c/o General Delivery
City, State, ZIP Code

Place the phrase "Hold for A.T. Hiker" (and your expected due date) in lower left corner of package or label.

WARNING!—Do not send maildrop packages to post offices via UPS or Federal Express, since postal personnel are prevented by law from accepting or holding such private-carrier packages.

The Thru-hiker's Planning Guide

List of Accommodations

Pack in MD#	Location (town and lodging facility)	# of nights	$ per night	Total $
START	Neels Gap, Walasiyi Ctr. Bunkroom	1	7.00	7.00
1	Wesser, NC, NOC Bunkroom	1	8.00	8.00
3	Hot Springs, NC, Jesuit Hostel	2	7.00	14.00
4	Erwin, TN, NRC Hostel	1	8.00	8.00
5	Damascus, VA, Hostel	2	2.00	4.00
5	Atkins, VA, Motel	1	16.00	16.00
7	Pearisburg, VA, Hostel	1	4.00	4.00
8	Troutville, VA, Motel	1	24.00	24.00
10	Harpers Ferry, WV, Hostel	1	20.00	20.00
10	Pine Grove Furnace St. Pk., Hostel	1	6.00	6.00
11	Duncannon, PA, Hotel	2	7.42	14.84
13	Delaware Water Gap, PA, Hostel	2	3.00	6.00
15	Upper Goose Pond Cabin	2	3.00	6.00
17	Kent Pond, B & B	1	10.00	10.00
18	Atwell Rd., DOC Cabin	1	5.00	5.00
19	Liberty Spring Campsite	1	4.00	4.00
19	Garfield Ridge Campsite	1	4.00	4.00
19	Ethan Pond Campsite	1	4.00	4.00
19	Lakes of the Clouds, Dungeon	1	6.00	6.00
19	Carter Notch AMC Hut	1	37.50	37.50
20	Gorham House Inn, Hostel	2	5.00	10.00
20	Speck Pond Shelter	1	4.00	4.00
21	Andover, ME, Hostel	1	8.00	8.00
22	Stratton, ME, Hotel	1	20.00	20.00
23	Monson, ME, Shaw's Boarding Home (incls. meals)	2	18.00	36.00
23	Daicey Pond Leantos	1	4.00	4.00

33 nites

Total Estimated Cost $290.34

Sample Planning Notebook

Budget Planner

		Grocery Stores			Restaurants							
	Budgeting for Meals Lodging etc.	Breakfasts @ $ 4 per meal	Lunches @ $ 3 per meal	Suppers @ $ 5 per meal	Breakfasts @ $ 5 per meal	Lunches @ $ 5 per meal	Suppers @ $ 8 per meal	Lodging costs (from List of Accommodations)	Miscellaneous expenses (estimate)	Fun money (estimate)		TOTALS (IN TRAVELER'S CHECKS)
MD#	Maildrop Location											
0	START OF HIKE	36	30	45				10	19			140
1	WESSER, NC				5		8	8	3	16		40
2	FONTANA DAM, NC	24	18	30			8		5	35		120
3	HOT SPRINGS, NC				10	10	16	14	5	25		80
4	ERWIN, TN	4			5		8	8	5	30		60
5	DAMASCUS, VA				15	10	24	20	5	66		140
6	BASTIAN, VA				5	5	8			42		60
7	PEARISBURG, VA				5	5	8	8	5	29		60
8	TROUTVILLE, VA				5	5	8	24	3	15		60
9	WAYNESBORO, VA				10	10	16		5	39		80
10	HARPERS FERRY, WV				5	5	16	26	5	23		80
11	DUNCANNON, PA				10	10	16	15	5	44		100
12	PORT CLINTON, PA				5	5				30		40
13	DELAWARE WATER GAP, PA				10	10	24	6	5	45		100
14	BEAR MOUNTAIN, NY				5					35		40
15	KENT, CT				5			6	5	44		60
16	CHESHIRE, MA				5	5	8		5	37		60
17	MANCHESTER CTR., VT				10	10	16	10	5	49		100
18	HANOVER, NH				10	10	16	5	5	54		100
19	GLENCLIFF, NH							56		44		100
20	GORHAM, NH				10	10	16	14	5	45		100
21	ANDOVER, ME				5	5	8	8	5	49		80
22	STRATTON, ME		3	5	5	5	8	20	3	31		80
23	MONSON, ME	8	6	10		10		40	5	41		120

Total Estimated Cost $ 2000.00

The Thru-hiker's Planning Guide

Back-up Gear List

Equipment:

1. Stove, MSR Whisperlite
2. Stove, Trangia Westwind
3. Stove, Zzip Sierra
4. Nalgene Fuel Bottle (1 pt.)
5. Water Filter Pump
6. Filter, replacement unit
7. Polar Pure (iodine)
8. Water Bottle (1 qt. WM)
9. Water Bottle (1 qt. Lexan)
10. Spout (spare for water bag)
11. Bladder (for water bag)
12. Stuff sack (16" x 8"⌀)
13. Stuff sack (18" x 7"⌀)
14. Eyeglasses (plastic lens)
15. Raincover (from old pack)
16. Skillet, stainless steel
17. Sleeping Bag, Summer 55°F
18. Thermarest, full-length
19. Sitting pad (spare)

Clothing/Footwear:

37. Boots, Vasque Clarion II
38. Boots, Vasque Highlander
39. Insoles, Spenco
40. Socks, Thorlo KX-11 (3 pr.)
41. Socks, Thorlo TKX-11 (3 pr.)
42. Sock Liners (2 pr.)
43. Rainpants, Sierra Designs
44. Ragg Sweater
45. Down Vest
46. Gloves, wool
47. Thermax underwear (heavy)
48. Wristwatch, Casio Therm.

Post Office Information

The post offices in this listing are the ones most frequently used as maildrops. Postal personnel in these offices are accustomed to dealing with thru-hiker mail and will usually hold general-delivery packages longer than the regulation 15 days (unless noted otherwise below), important should you fall behind schedule. Post offices not in this listing may not extend this courtesy. The number preceding the post-office name indicates how many thru-hikers used that location last year, as follows: ❶ = 100+, ❷ = 50+, ❸ = 25+. Note that most post offices ask for a photo I.D. when you claim general-delivery mail.

❷ **Suches, GA 30572**—Mon-Fri 7:30-noon and 1-4:30, Sat 7:30-11:30; 706-747-2611

❸ **Hiawassee, GA 30546**—Mon-Fri 8:30-5 (closes Wed 12:30), Sat 8:30-12:30; 706-896-3632

❷ **Franklin, NC 28734**—Mon-Fri 8-5:10, Sat 9-noon; 704-524-3219

❶ **Fontana Dam, NC 28733**—Mon-Fri 8:30-noon and 1-5, Sat 10-noon; 704-498-2315

❷ **Gatlinburg, TN 37738**—Mon-Fri 9-5, Sat 10-noon; 615-436-5464

❶ **Hot Springs, NC 28743**—Mon-Fri 8:30-11:30 and 12:30-4:15, Sat 9-11; 704-622-3242

❶ **Erwin, TN 37650**—Mon-Fri 8-5, Sat 10-noon; anyone working will answer buzzer at rear of PO after hours; 615-743-4811

❷ **Roan Mountain, TN 37687**—Mon-Fri 8-11:30 and 12:30-4:30, Sat 8-11; 615-772-3661

❸ **Elk Park, NC 28622**—Mon-Fri 7:30-noon and 1:15-4:30, Sat 7:30-10:30; 704-733-5711

❷ **Hampton, TN 37658**—Mon-Fri 7:30-4:30, Sat 8-10; 615-725-3703

❶ **Damascus, VA 24236**—Mon-Fri 8:30-1:30 and 2-4:30, Sat 8:30-11; 703-475-3411

❸ **Troutdale, VA 24378**—Mon-Fri 8-noon and 1-5, Sat 8-11; 703-677-3221

❶ **Atkins, VA 24311**—Mon-Fri 8-12:30 and 1:30-5, Sat 8-11; 703-783-5551

❶ **Bastian, VA 24314**—Mon-Fri 8-noon and 12:30-4:30, Sat 8-10:30; 703-688-4631

❷ **Bland, VA 24315**—Mon-Fri 8-11:30 and noon-4, Sat 8-11; 703-688-3751

❶ **Pearisburg, VA 24134**—Mon-Fri 8:30-5, Sat 8:30-noon; will answer knock 6am-6pm weekdays; 703-921-1100

❷ **Catawba, VA 24070**—Mon-Fri 8-noon and 1-5, Sat 8-10:30; 703-384-6011

❶ **Troutville, VA 24175**—Mon-Fri 8:30-5, Sat 8:30-11:30; 703-992-1472

❸ **Cloverdale, VA 24077**—Mon-Fri 8-noon and 1-5, Sat 9-noon; 703-992-2334

❷ **Big Island, VA 24526**—Mon-Fri 8-12:30 and 1:30-5, Sat 8-11; 804-299-5072

❷ **Glasgow, VA 24555**—Mon-Fri 8-4:30, Sat 8-11; 703-258-2852

❷ **Montebello. VA 24464**—Mon-Fri 8-noon and 12:30-4:30, Sat 9-11:30; 703-377-9218

❶ **Tyro, VA 22976**—Mon-Sat 6am-8pm (see note in text); 804-277-9401

❶ **Waynesboro, VA 22980**—Mon-Fri 8:30-5, Sat 9-11; 703-949-8129

❷ **Front Royal, VA 22630**—Mon-Fri 8:30-5, Sat 8:30-2; 703-635-4540

❷ **Linden, VA 22642**—Mon-Fri 8-noon and 1-5, Sat 8-noon; will hold packages for 15 days maximum; 703-636-9936

❶ **Harpers Ferry, WV 25425**—Mon-Fri 8-4, Sat 9-noon; 304-535-2479

❸ **South Mountain, PA 17261**—Mon-Fri 8-noon and 1-5, Sat 8-noon; 717-749-5833

❶ **Boiling Springs, PA 17007**—Mon-Fri 8-1 and 2-4:30, Sat 8-noon; 717-258-6668

❶ **Duncannon, PA 17020**—Mon-Fri 8-4:30, Wed until 5:30, Sat 8-noon; 717-834-3332

❶ **Port Clinton, PA 19549**—Mon-Fri 7:30-12:30 and 2-5, Sat 8-11; 610-562-3787

❸ **Slatington, PA 18080**—Mon-Fri 8:30-5, Sat 8:30-noon; 610-767-2182

❸ **Palmerton, PA 18071**—Mon-Fri 8:30-5, Sat 8:30-noon; 610-826-2286

❶ **Delaware Water Gap, PA 18327**—Mon-Fri 8:30-12:15 and 1:30-5, Sat 8:30-11; 717-476-0304

❷ **Unionville, NY 10988**—Mon-Fri 8-noon and 1-5, Sat 8-noon; 914-726-3535
❸ **Glenwood, NJ 07418**—Mon-Fri 8-5, Sat 8-noon; 201-764-7280
❸ **Vernon, NJ 07462**—Mon-Fri 8:30-5, Sat 8:30-2:30; 201-764-2920
❷ **Arden, NY 10910**—Mon-Fri 8-noon and 1-5, Sat 8-noon; 914-351-5341
❶ **Bear Mountain, NY 10911**—Mon-Fri 7:30-1 and 2:30-5, Sat 7:30-11:30; 914-786-3747
❸ **Fort Montgomery, NY 10922**—Mon-Fri 8:30-5, Sat 8:30-noon; 914-446-2173
❸ **Pawling, NY 12564**—Mon-Fri 8:30-5, Sat 9-noon; 914-855-1010
❶ **Kent, CT 06757**—Mon-Fri 8-1 and 2-5, Sat 8-12:30; 203-927-3435
❷ **Cornwall Bridge, CT 06754**—Mon-Fri 8-1 and 2-5, Sat 9-12:30; 203-672-6710
❸ **Falls Village, CT 06031**—Mon-Fri 8-1 and 2-5, Sat 8-noon; 203-824-7781
❷ **Salisbury, CT 06068**—Mon-Fri 8-1 and 2-5, Sat 9-noon; 203-435-9485
❸ **South Egremont, MA 01258**—Mon-Fri 7:45-5, Sat 7:45-1; 413-528-1571
❷ **Tyringham, MA 01264**—Mon-Fri 8:30-11 and 4-5:30, Sat 8:30-12:30; or call 413-243-0419 for between-hours pickup; 413-243-1225
❷ **Dalton, MA 01226**—Mon-Fri 8-5, Sat 8-noon; 413-684-0364
❶ **Cheshire, MA 01225**—Mon-Fri 8-1 and 2-5, Sat 8-noon; 413-743-3184
❸ **North Adams, MA 01247**—Mon-Fri 8:30-4:30, Sat 10-noon; will answer back door until 4pm on Sat; 413-664-4554
❸ **Williamstown, MA 01267**—Mon-Fri 8:30-4:30, Sat 9:30-12:30; 413-458-3707
❸ **Bennington, VT 05201**—Mon-Fri 8:30-4:30, Sat 8:30-noon; 802-442-2421
❶ **Manchester Center, VT 05255**—Mon-Fri 8:30-5, Sat 9-1; 802-362-3070
❸ **Killington, VT 05751**—Mon-Fri 8-4:30, Sat 8-noon; 802-775-4247
❸ **South Pomfret, VT 05067**—Mon-Fri 8:30-5:30, Sat 8:30-12:30; 802-457-1147
❸ **West Hartford, VT 05084**—Mon-Fri 7:45-11:45 and 1-5, Sat 7:45-10:45; 802-295-6293
❷ **Norwich, VT 05055**—Mon-Fri 8:30-5, Sat 9-noon; 802-649-1608
❶ **Hanover, NH 03755**—Mon-Fri 8:30-5, Sat 8:30-noon; knock at side door for pickup until 5:30pm weekdays; 603-643-4544
❶ **Glencliff, NH 03238**—Mon-Fri 7-10 and 2-5, Sat 7-1; 603-989-5858
❷ **North Woodstock, NH 03262**—Mon-Fri 8-12:30 and 1:30-5, Sat 8-noon; 603-745-8134
❸ **Mt. Washington, NH 03589**—M-F 10:30-5, Sat 10:30-12:30; open only if weather permits access to summit, not recommended as maildrop: 603-846-5404
❶ **Gorham, NH 03581**—Mon-Fri 8:30-5, Sat 8-noon; 603-466-2182
❷ **Andover, ME 04216**—Mon-Fri 8:30-1:30 and 2-4:45, Sat 9-12:15; 207-392-4571
❶ **Rangeley, ME 04970**—Mon-Fri 8:30-5, Sat 8:30-noon; 207-864-2233
❶ **Stratton, ME 04982**—Mon-Fri 8-12:30 and 1:45-5, Sat 8-11:45; 207-246-6461
❶ **Caratunk, ME 04925**—Mon-Fri 8-noon and 12:30-4:30, Sat 8-noon; 207-672-5532
❶ **Monson, ME 04464**—Mon-Fri 8-11:30 and 12:30-5, Sat 8-noon; 207-997-3975

IMPORTANT!

Do not send UPS or FedEx packages to post offices, since regulations prevent postal personnel from accepting and holding private-carrier packages.

Table of Town Services

Symbols: • = in town, N = in nearby town, B = on local bus route, ? = sometimes open															
TOWN SERVICES	POST OFFICE	HOSTEL	MOTEL/HOTEL	BED & BREAKFAST	RESTAURANT	FAST FOODS	SUPERMARKET	GROCERY STORE	LAUNDROMAT	COLEMAN BY PINT	OUTFITTER	COBBLER	BANK	PHARMACY	HARDWARE STORE
Suches, Ga	•							•							
Hiawassee, GA	•		•		•	•	•	•	•	•					
Franklin, NC	•		•		•	•	•	•	•				•	•	•
Fontana Dam, NC	•	•	•		•	•		•	•	•					
Gatlinburg, TN	•		•		•	•	•	•	•	•	•		•	•	•
Hot Springs, NC	•	•	•	•	•			•	•				•		
Erwin, TN	•	•	•	•	•	•	•	•	•	?		•	•	•	•
Roan Mountain, TN	•	•	•		•	•		•	•				•		•
Elk Park, NC	•		•		•			?							•
Hampton, TN	•	•	•		•	•	•	•		•			•		•
Damascus, VA	•	•	N	?	•	•	N	•	•	•	•	•	•	•	•
Troutdale, VA	•				•	•		•		•			•		
Atkins, VA	•		•		•			•	•						•
Bastian, VA	•	•			•			•		•					
Bland, VA	•		•		•	•		•	•				•	•	•
Pearisburg, VA	•	•	•		•	•	•	•	•	•		•	•	•	•
Catawba, VA	•				•			•		•					
Troutville, VA	•		•		•	•	•	•	•	•			•	•	•
Cloverdale, VA	•	•								•					
Big Island, VA	•					•		•							
Glasgow, VA	•				•		•		•				•		•
Montebello, VA	•		•		?					•					
Tyro, VA	•							•		•					
Waynesboro, VA	•	•			•	•	•	•	•	•	•	•	•	•	•
Front Royal, VA	•		•		•	•	•	•	•				•	•	•
Linden, VA	•							•							
Harpers Ferry, WV	•		•	?	•	B	B	B	B	•			•	B	B
South Mountain, PA	•				•			•							
Boiling Springs, PA	•			•	•			•			N		•		
Duncannon, PA	•		•		•		•		•	•	N		•	•	•
Port Clinton, PA	•	•	•		•	N	N	N	N		N		N	N	N
Slatington, PA	•		•		•			•	•	•			•	•	•
Palmerton, PA	•	•	•		•		•	•	•				•	•	•
Delaware Water Gap, PA	•	•	B		•	B	B	B	•	•	B	B	B	B	

85

Table of Town Services

Symbols: ● = in town, N = in nearby town, B = on local bus route, ? = sometimes open

TOWN SERVICES	POST OFFICE	HOSTEL	MOTEL/HOTEL	BED & BREAKFAST	RESTAURANT	FAST FOODS	SUPERMARKET	GROCERY STORE	LAUNDROMAT	COLEMAN BY PINT	OUTFITTER	COBBLER	BANK	PHARMACY	HARDWARE STORE
Unionville, NY	●				●			●							
Glenwood, NJ	●			●				●							
Vernon, NJ	●	●	●		●	●	●	●	●					●	
Arden, NY	●							?							
Bear Mountain, NY	●		●		●	N	N	N	N				N	N	N
Fort Montgomery, NY	●		●		●	●	N	●	N				N	N	N
Pawling, NY	●	●					●		●						
Kent, CT	●		●		●	●		●	●	●			●	●	●
Cornwall Bridge, CT	●		●					●							
Falls Village, CT	●				●								●		
Salisbury, CT	●			●	●			●	●			N	●	●	●
South Egremont, MA	●			●	●			●							
Tyringham, MA	●			●											
Dalton, MA	●		●		●	●		●	●				●	●	●
Cheshire, MA	●	●	B	●	●	●	B	●	B	●	B		●	B	●
North Adams, MA	●		●		●	●	●	●	●			●	●	●	●
Williamstown, MA	●		●	●	●	●	●	●	●	●			●	●	●
Bennington, VT	●		●	●	●	●	●	●	●	●		●	●	●	●
Manchester Center, VT	●	●	●	●	●	●	●	●	●	●	●	●	●	●	●
Killington, VT	●		●					●							
South Pomfret, VT	●							●							
West Hartford, VT	●														
Norwich, VT	●			●	●										
Hanover, NH	●	?	●		●	●	●	●	●	●	●	●	●	●	●
Glencliff, NH	●			N			N	N							
North Woodstock, NH	●		●	●	●		●	●	●	●	N		N	N	●
Mt. Washington, NH	●					●									
Gorham, NH	●	●	●	●	●	●	●	●	●	●	●	N	●	●	●
Andover, ME	●	●		●	●			●		●					●
Rangeley, ME	●		●	●	●	●	●	●	●	●	?		●	●	●
Stratton, ME	●		●		●	●		●	●	●			●		●
Caratunk, ME	●							●							
Monson, ME	●	●		●	●	●		●	●	●					
Millinocket, ME	●		●	●	●	●	●	●	●				●	●	●

Climate and Weather Chart

MONTHLY AVERAGES	1st line: Average max./min. temperature in degrees Fahrenheit 2nd line: Average rain/snow in inches, T = trace 3rd line: Average number of days with some precipitation											
Location	JAN	FEB	MCH	APR	MAY	JUN	JUL	AUG	SEP	OCT	NOV	DEC
BAXTER STATE PARK, Maine Elevation: 1,000	24/5 3/23 12	27/6 3/24 10	35/17 3/15 12	48/29 3/4 11	62/33 3/T 11	71/47 4/T 10	78/54 4/0 10	76/51 4/T 10	65/44 3/0 10	55/33 4/T 9	40/26 5/6 10	27/10 3/15 11
PINKHAM NOTCH, New Hampshire Elevation: 2,000	27/7 1/35 13	28/7 1/34 12	35/16 2/36 14	47/28 3/20 14	61/39 5/2 13	69/48 5/T 12	74/53 5/0 10	72/51 4/T 11	64/44 5/T 10	55/35 5/2 10	41/24 4/15 11	29/11 2/28 12
MT. WASHINGTON, New Hampshire Elevation: 6,252	14/-2 2/29 14	14/-2 2/32 13	19/4 3/33 14	31/17 3/25 15	36/23 5/10 14	51/39 6/1 14	53/42 6/T 12	54/43 7/T 11	44/34 7/2 11	30/16 5/10 11	27/14 4/24 13	17/1 3/33 14
SHERBURNE PASS, Vermont Elevation: 2,100	24/5 T/23 14	25/6 0/25 12	33/15 1/16 13	47/28 2/5 13	61/37 3/T 13	70/47 3/0 11	74/52 3/0 12	73/49 3/0 12	65/41 3/0 11	55/33 3/T 11	40/24 2/7 14	26/10 1/19 14
CHESHIRE, Massachusetts Elevation: 1,150	30/12 1/17 12	32/14 1/19 10	39/22 2/13 12	53/33 4/5 11	66/43 4/0 10	75/52 4/0 10	79/56 5/0 11	78/55 4/T 10	69/47 4/0 10	59/37 3/T 9	46/29 3/6 11	33/17 2/13 12
BEAR MOUNTAIN, New York Elevation: 1,300	32/18 2/11 12	33/19 1/14 10	43/27 3/9 12	55/38 4/T 11	66/48 5/0 11	75/57 4/0 10	79/63 6/0 12	77/61 4/0 10	70/54 4/0 9	60/44 3/T 9	47/33 5/1 9	35/22 3/13 10
DELAWARE WATER GAP, Pennsylvania Elevation: 400	32/17 2/14 12	33/16 2/13 11	42/22 3/12 12	55/34 1/3 11	67/44 4/T 11	75/52 5/0 10	78/58 5/0 11	75/57 5/0 11	70/49 5/T 8	62/40 5/T 8	48/30 3/5 9	34/19 3/8 10
DUNCANNON, Pennsylvania Elevation: 340	38/24 2/8 13	41/26 2/7 12	49/31 3/7 12	64/42 3/T 11	75/52 4/T 12	83/61 3/T 10	87/65 3/0 11	85/63 3/0 10	78/56 3/0 9	67/45 3/T 8	52/35 3/2 9	41/26 2/6 11
HARPERS FERRY, West Virginia Elevation: 500	41/25 2/5 11	44/27 2/4 10	51/31 3/6 12	63/40 3/T 11	74/50 4/T 12	82/59 4/0 11	86/63 4/0 11	84/61 4/0 11	78/54 3/T 8	67/43 3/T 8	53/34 3/1 9	42/26 2/5 10
SHENANDOAH NATL. PARK, Virginia Elevation: 3,500	39/20 3/8 12	40/21 2/7 11	47/26 3/8 11	59/37 4/2 12	67/46 5/T 11	74/54 5/0 10	76/57 5/0 10	75/56 6/0 11	69/50 5/T 10	60/41 5/1 9	49/30 3/3 10	39/22 3/7 11
DAMASCUS, Virginia Elevation: 2,600	44/24 3/7 12	45/24 3/6 11	52/30 4/7 11	63/39 4/2 11	70/46 4/T 10	77/54 5/0 11	79/58 5/0 10	79/57 4/0 10	74/50 3/0 9	66/40 3/1 9	54/31 3/2 10	44/26 3/6 12
HOT SPRINGS, North Carolina Elevation: 1,400	48/28 3/7 13	49/29 3/8 12	55/33 4/8 13	64/40 4/1 12	71/48 5/T 11	78/55 5/0 11	79/58 6/0 11	79/57 6/T 10	77/51 4/0 10	68/42 4/1 9	56/32 3/2 11	49/28 3/7 13
NEWFOUND GAP (GSMNP), Tennessee Elevation: 5,000	37/13 5/22 12	40/14 4/20 11	47/20 5/13 12	57/28 5/4 11	65/36 5/T 11	72/44 5/T 11	74/45 6/0 11	73/46 5/0 10	69/40 3/T 9	59/29 3/T 8	47/18 3/3 9	38/13 4/9 11
SPRINGER MOUNTAIN, Georgia Elevation: 3,300	44/19 5/1 12	46/31 6/1 11	52/25 6/1 11	63/34 4/T 10	69/42 4/0 10	75/50 4/0 11	77/52 5/0 13	77/52 4/0 12	73/45 3/0 9	63/33 3/0 8	53/24 3/0 9	45/19 5/1 12

Note: Add or subtract 3.5 degrees for each 1,000 feet of elevation change to arrive at approximations of temperature averages for other nearby locations on the Trail route.

Trail Food Calorie Chart

This chart gives calorie ratings for some of the bulk foods and brand-name products commonly used by thru-hikers, and can be used to approximate the calories in your Trail meals. Calorie ratings per ounce of weight are shown unless noted otherwise. An average calorie rating is given for brand-name processed-food products which have multiple flavors but essentially the same ingredients in each.

Almonds, raw *(per oz.)*	162
Bagels *(per large bagel)*	300
Beans, quick-cook *(per dry oz.)*	105
Beef, canned *(per 5oz. can)*	320
Beef, dried *(per oz.)*	60
Bisquick mix *(per oz.)*	120
(per 5.5oz. pkg.)	300
Bread, loaf *(average per slice)*	70
Bread, pita *(average per pita)*	130
Bread, English muffin *(per muffin)*	140
Breakfast bars *(per bar)*	200
Candies *(average per oz.)*	110
Candy bars *(regular size bar)*	280
Cereals *(average per dry oz.)*	120
Cheeses, white *(per 3oz. pkg.)*	300
Cheeses, yellow *(per oz.)*	110
Cheesecake mix *(per 11oz. pkg.)*	1360
Chicken, canned *(per 5oz. can)*	200
Chocolate *(per oz.)*	140
Cocoa mix, instant *(per pkg.)*	110
Coffee, instant *(per dry oz.)*	2
Cookies *(average per oz.)*	140
Crackers *(average per oz.)*	160
Cream of wheat, instant *(per pkg.)*	100
English muffins *(per muffin)*	140
Freeze-dried foods	*
Fruits, dried *(average per oz.)*	80
Fruit rollups *(per roll)*	100
Flours, all types *(per oz.)*	95
Gatorade, with sugar *(per dry oz.)*	110
(per 4.6oz. pkg.)	500
Gorp *(raisins, peanuts, M&Ms; per oz.)*	130
Granola cereals *(average per oz.)*	100
Granola bars *(per 1oz. bar)*	120
Gravy mixes *(per 0.8oz. pkg.)*	60
Grits, instant *(per 1oz. pkg.)*	100
Ham, canned *(per 5oz. can)*	475
Honey *(per oz.)*	85
Instant-breakfast mix *(per pkg)*	130
Jams *(per oz.)*	80
Jello gelatin *(per 3oz. pkg.)*	320
Jelly *(per oz.)*	80
Jerky, all types *(per oz.)*	60
Kool-Aid, with sugar *(per oz.)*	110
(per 5.5oz. pkg.)	550
Kudos bars *(per bar)*	200
Lipton Pasta & Sauce dinner *(per pkg.)*	520
(with milk and margarine)	800
Lipton Rice & Sauce dinner *(per pkg.)*	520
(with margarine)	600
Macaroni, dry *(per oz.)*	105
Mac and cheese dinner *(per pkg.)*	760
(with milk and margarine)	1160
Margarine, squeeze-type *(per oz.)*	160
Milk, lowfat powdered *(per dry oz.)*	90
(per 1 qt. pkg.)	320
Minute Rice *(per dry oz.)*	100
Nuts, raw *(average per oz.)*	170
Nuts, roasted in oil *(per oz.)*	175
Oatmeal, instant *(per pkg.)*	120
Oils, liquid cooking *(per oz. wt.)*	250
Pancake mix *(per dry oz.)*	100
Pasta, all types *(per dry oz.)*	105
Peanut butter *(per oz.)*	160
Peanuts, roasted in oil *(per oz.)*	162
Peanuts, dry-roasted *(per oz.)*	160
Peas, quick-cook *(per dry oz.)*	105
Pop-Tarts *(per pkg. of 2)*	400
Postum, unmixed *(per oz.)*	4
Potatoes, instant *(per dry oz.)*	90
Pudding mix, instant *(per 2oz. pkg.)*	180
Raisins *(per oz.)*	80
Ramen noodles *(per pkg.)*	400
Rice, all types *(per dry oz.)*	100
Rice-A-Roni *(per dry oz.)*	105
Rice cakes *(per cake)*	35
Sardines, packed in oil *(per tin)*	480
Sausages *(average per oz.)*	100
Soups, instant *(per pkg)*	80
Spaghetti *(per dry oz.)*	105
Stove-Top Stuffing *(per dry oz.)*	120
Tuna, in water *(per 3oz. can)*	96
(per 6oz. can)	200
Tuna, in oil *(per 3oz. can)*	230
(per 6oz. can)	465
Vienna sausages *(small can)*	300

---

* Freeze-dried foods
Calorie ratings for freeze-dried dinners may be requested from the manufacturer, or you can approximate the calorie rating by multiplying the dry weight in ounces by 125 calories per ounce.

Thru-hiker's Product Guide

This section contains information about items of gear most frequently used and recommended by recent A.T. thru-hikers, and includes information about new items that should prove popular. Items are listed alphabetically by category and randomly by brand name. Descriptions are based on information supplied by the manufacturer and verified by the on-Trail observations of your author. Though you may choose to use gear not mentioned in this section, take note of the listed models and the features that make these items so suitable for use on a thru-hike. Use the information to guide you in the selection of products for use on your hike.

At the end of this section, addresses and telephone numbers of manufacturers and distributors of backpacking products are provided, so that you can write or call for brochures and catalogues as you do your product research. When you contact a company, be sure to mention that you are preparing for a thru-hike and need information promptly, since some companies can take months to put you on their regular mailing list. You might also mention that you got their name from this guide, which may speed their response ... but it may not!

Backpacks

JanSport *Yosemite*: external-frame, 4600 cu. in., 5lbs. 3oz., flexible aluminum anatomical frame with no welds, detachable dual-density hip belt with quick release buckle, flexible Velocity hip-arm suspension system with four-position adjustment for varying loads and terrain, curved shoulder straps with adjustable sternum strap, ventilated back pad, detachable packbag with two zippered panel-loading main compartments and five zippered accessory pockets, map pocket, outside water-bottle pocket, tent-pole sleeve, and outside compression straps, frame and suspension system fully adjustable in minutes without tools; for hikers 5'6"-6'4" in height; *Bryce* an identical, but slightly smaller, model for shorter hikers 4'10"-5'8" in height. Other popular models made by JanSport include the *D-series* packs which have similar features.

Kelty *Radial Light XLT*: external-frame, 3500 cu. in. extendable to 5535 cu.in, 6lbs. 6oz., telescoping rigid aluminum frame with welded-joint construction, adjustable to torsos from 12in. to 21in., three-layer one-piece waist belt, wide curved shoulder straps with adjustable load lifters, ventilated back bands, detachable packbag with top-loading upper compartment, zippered panel-loading lower compartment, zippered divider between upper and lower compartments, four zippered side pockets, map pocket, outside water-bottle pocket, and outside compression straps; available in a women's model. Other popular models made by Kelty include the *Radial Sherpa XLT* and the *Super Tioga*.

Camp Trails *Wilderness*: external-frame, 4200 cu. in. for panel-loading model, 3780-4780 cu. in. for top-loading model, both about 6lbs. 2oz., rigid aluminum frame with welded-joint construction, four-layer laminated one-piece waist belt with torso and terrain adjustments, curved wrap-around shoulder straps with adjustable sternum strap, top-loading model has two compartments with pass-through sides and outside zippered access to the bottom compartment, panel-loading model has two zippered main compartments, both have large and small side pockets, a water-bottle pocket, an outside "kitchen-sink" pocket on the lower rear panel for storing frequently used items, and compression straps. Other popular models made by Camp Trails include the *Denali* and *Teton*.

Gregory *Robson*: internal-frame, 5525-5925 cu. in., top-loading Cordura packbag with slight "V"-shaped flexible carbon-fiber stays and other features to provide maximum head clearance, Flo-Form harness system with shaped shoulder straps, sculpted back pads with air-flo ventilation channels, lumbar pad to provide extra cushioning to the lower back area, zippered access to main compartment, releasable internal dividers and compression straps to stabilize and organize gear in the main compartment, high-performance padded hip belt, large sleeping-bag compartment with zippered access, stretch-mesh hip pockets, removable top pocket that converts to a fanny pack, and compression straps. Other popular models made by Gregory include the *Denali*, *Massif*, and *Wind River*; the new *Ranier*, a very large capacity pack, should prove popular for winter thru-hikes.

Dana Design *Terraplane*: internal-frame, available in extra-small to extra-large models with volumes of 5340-6300 cu. in. and weights of 6lbs. 0oz. to 6lbs. 15oz., top-loading Cordura pack bag with ArcFlex system of aluminum and carbon-fiber stays and plastic framesheet designed to support the weight of the pack load without depending on the load to provide structural support and without working against the wearer's own movement, concave wedge in top of pack to allow full head movement, contoured hip belt and shoulder pads available in all sizes, lumbar padding backed by framesheet to distribute weight uniformly across the back, top-loading main compartment with zippered lower sleeping-bag compartment, horizontal divider to keep load out of the bottom of pack bag, retractable bottom to give space for strapping on external gear or reducing pack volume, two large outside zippered pockets, and removable pack lid that combines with the removable hip belt to make a hipsac.

Mountainsmith *Delta Elite*: internal-frame, available in three sizes with volumes of 4984-7997 cu. in. and weights of 5lbs. 12oz. to 6lbs. 7 oz., combination top- and panel-loading Cordura pack bag with Infinity suspension system featuring load-transfer struts to lift the pack off the shoulders and transfer the weight evenly between the lumbar region and waist belt, infinitely adjustable shoulder straps, built-in measuring tape to precisely adjust belt to any waist size, zippered panel to provide access to main compartment, two bellows pockets accessible from either side, unique trampoline-like pocket for stowing wet gear, lower mesh side pockets, compression straps, and removable top pocket that converts to a fanny pack or shoulder bag. Other popular models made by Mountainsmith include the *Delta Alpine Frostfire* series.

Other: Although not quite as frequently seen on the A.T. as those listed above, several brands and models that deserve mention are Lowe's *Contour IV* internal-frame pack, The North Face's *Snow Leopard II* internal-frame pack, REI's *Wonderland* external-frame pack, and the McHale & Company *Alpineer I & II* internal-frame packs custom-made to the user's torso measurements.

The Thru-hiker's Planning Guide

Boots

All models listed below are suitable for use on a thru-hike, although all models may not be suitable for your use. Since boots come in an endless variety of styles, specific features are omitted. The most popular models among recent A.T. thru-hikers are indicated by an asterisk (*). The letters "wp" in parenthesis following a model name means that it is rated as waterproof.

Vasque offers all four types of boots seen on the A.T. in a full range of styles and features. Some of the popular boot models by Vasque include the lightweight fabric/leather *Clarion III*; the medium-weight fabric/leather *Clarion II**, *Clarion V* (wp), *Voyager* (wp)*, *Skywalk II* (wp)*, and *Trailwalk* (wp); the medium-weight leather *Clarion IV**, *Escape* (wp)*, *Sundowner* (wp)*, *Newbrier* (wp), *Eclipse* (wp)*, *Summit* (wp)*, *Super Hiker II*, and *Trek*; and the heavyweight leather *Montana* and *Vagabond II*.

Merrell offers all types of boots seen on the A.T., except the heavyweight leathers, in a full range of styles and features. Some of the popular boot models by Merrell include the lightweight fabric/leather *Horizon*, *Solo**, *Light Traveler**, and *Ridge Runner**; the medium-weight fabric/leather *Extreme*, *Lazer**, *Timberline**, *Zephyr* (wp)*, and *Blazer* (wp)*; and the medium-weight leather *Canyon WTC*, *Cumbrian WTC*, *Wilderness**, and *Guide**.

Danner offers medium-weight fabric/leather and medium-weight leather boots in a full range of styles and features used on the A.T. Some of the popular boot models by Danner include the medium-weight fabric/leather *Trail Spirit* (wp)*, *Mountain Spirit* (wp)*, *Free Spirit* (wp)*, *Santiam*, *Explorer* (wp)*, *Mt. Hood* (wp), and *Danner Light* (wp)*; and the medium-weight leather *Trekker* (wp)*, *Midnight Trekker* (wp), *Broken Top**, and *Mountain Light* (wp)*.

Raichle offers all types of boots seen on the A.T., except heavyweight leathers, in a full range of styles and features. Some of the popular boot models by Raichle include the lightweight fabric/leather *Wasatch* and *Telluride*; the medium-weight fabric/leather *Strada*, *Brava*, *Sawtooth*, *Explorer*, *Scout*, and *Sierra**; and the medium-weight leather *Olympic*, *Helvitica**, *Ranier**, *Verbier**, *Ranger**, *Tibet Sirdar* (wp), *Burma* (wp)*, *Alpin Trekker**, *Super Trekker*, *Palue*, and *Monte Rosa**.

Hi-Tec Sports offers all types of boots seen on the A.T., except heavyweight leathers, in a full range of styles and features. Some of the popular boot models by Hi-Tec Sports include the lightweight fabric/leather *Sierra Lite*, *Sierra Low**, *Shasta*, and *Teton**; the medium-weight fabric/leather *Badlands*, *Yazoo*, *Voyageur*, *Class V Suede*, *Logan**, *Mauna Kea**, and *Gannett Peak**; and the medium-weight leather *Rogue**, *Class V Leather**, *Katahdin**, and *McKinley*.

Tecnica offers all types of boots seen on the A.T., except heavyweight leathers, in a full range of styles and features. Some of the popular boot models by Tecnica include the lightweight fabric/leather *TKL*; the medium-weight fabric/leather *Tuscany GTX* (wp), *Mesa*, and *Cervino Super GTX* (wp)*; and the medium-weight leather *Teton* (wp)*, *Acadia* (wp)*, *Sasslong**, and *Cortina**.

One Sport offers all types of boots seen on the A.T., except heavyweight leathers, in a full range of styles and features. Some of the popular boot models by One Sport include the lightweight fabric/leather *Sundance* and *Cirque**; the medium-weight fabric/leather *Base Camp*; and the medium-weight leather *Chaparral**, *Tarn*, *Arete**, *Talus*, and *Moraine**.

Peter Limmer & Sons offers hand-made heavyweight leather boots custom fitted to the user's foot measurements. Orders must be placed at least six months in advance.

Sleeping Bags

Caribou Mountaineering offers synthetic-fill three-and four-season bags in mummy, modified-mummy, and rectangular styles, with temperature ratings from -30°F to 25°F. Fill materials used are Primaloft, Micro-loft, and Polarguard. Popular models made by Caribou include the Primaloft *3-Season*, *Winter*, and *Light Tour*; the Micro-loft *Early Frost*, *Cold Snap*, *Starry Night*, and *Warm Front*; and the Polarguard *Comet* and *Meteor*.

Kelty offers synthetic-fill three- and four-season bags in mummy, modified-mummy, and rectangular styles, with temperature ratings from -15°F to 55°F. Fill materials used are LiteLoft, Polarguard, Quallofil, and Hollofil. Popular models made by Kelty include the *Soft Touch LiteLoft*, *Silver Streak*, *Polaris*, *Clear Creek*, and *Philmont*. The 45°F *Le Tour* and 55°F *Light Top* are excellent choices as summer bags, two of only three truly hot-weather bags offered by any major manufacturer.

Sierra Designs offers synthetic-fill three- and four-season bags in mummy and modified-mummy styles, with temperature ratings from -15°F to 30°F. Fill material used in all bags is LiteLoft. Popular models made by Sierra Designs include the *Summerlite*, *Lite 'N Up*, *Varilite*, *Waylite*, and *Northernlite*.

Marmot offers down three- and four-season bags in mummy and modified-mummy styles, with temperature ratings from -40°F to 25°F. Fill material used includes 550- and 650-fill-power down. Popular models made by Marmot include the *Quail*, *Grouse*, *Osprey*, *Rhea*, *Swift*, *Nighthawk*, *Peregrine*, and *Kestrel*. Some models are available with a Gore-Tex shell that aids in heat retention, especially in windy conditions.

The North Face offers synthetic-fill and down three- and four-season bags in mummy and modified-mummy styles, with temperature ratings from -30°F to 35°F. Fill materials used are Polarguard HV and 550- and 650-fill-power down. Popular models made by The North Face include the Polarguard HV *Heatwave*, *Moondance*, *Littlefoot*, *Cat's Meow*, *Yetl*, *Snowshoe*, and *Manatee*; and the down-filled *Dunlin*, *Foxfire*, *Lightrider*, *Chrysalis*, and *Blue Kazoo*.

Moonstone offers synthetic-fill and down three- and four-season bags in mummy and modified-mummy styles, with temperature ratings from -30°F to 30°F. Fill materials used are LiteLoft, Polarguard HV, and 650-fill-power (or greater) down. Popular models made by Moonstone include the down-filled *Liberty Ridge II*, *PCT II*, *Spectrum II*, *Muir Trail*, and *Horizon*; the LiteLoft *Optima*, *Minima*, *Upside Down*, *Nitelite*, and *Starlite*; and the Polargurad HV *Gila*, *Iguana*, *Gecko*, and *Chameleon*.

Carinthia (Gold-Eck of Austria) offers synthetic-fill three- and four-season bags in mummy and modified-mummy styles, with temperature ratings from -40°F to 25°F. Fill material used is GLT, a European synthetic down. Popular models made by Gold-Eck include the *Mediterranee*, *Europe*, *Tundra*, *Husky Range*, *Husky Liberty*, and *Interrail*.

Wiggy's offers synthetic-fill three- and four-season bags in mummy and rectangular styles, with temperature ratings from -20°F to 40°F. Fill material used is Lamilite, a special insulation that allows bag construction without quilting. Popular models made by Wiggy's include the *Ultra Light*, *Super Light*, *Nautilus*, and *The Desert Bag*, a true hot-weather bag.

REI offers synthetic-fill and down three- and four-season bags in mummy, modified-mummy, and rectangular styles, with temperature ratings from -20°F to 35°F. Fill materials used are LiteLoft, Hollofil II, Quallofil, and 550-fill-power down. Popular models made by REI include the *Down Time*, *Nomad*, *Nod Pod*, *Radiator*, and *Starlite*.

Other: Some sleeping bag models made by Slumberjack, Coleman, and Feathered Friends have proven popular with past thru-hikers, but these manufacturers did not respond to requests for data about their products and verifiable information about product availability in 1994 could not be obtained prior to publication.

Stoves

MSR *Whisperlite*: white-gas stove, available in multi-fuel model, weighs 13.5oz., requires some setup and priming, detachable 22oz. fuel bottle and pump, burns 100 minutes on full fuel tank, brings a pint of water to a boil in about 4 minutes, boils 28 pints of water per pint of fuel, good stability, comes with wind screen, cleaning and maintenance kit optional but recommended. Other popular models made by MSR include the multi-fuel *XGK II*; the isobutane-fuel *Rapid Fire* has worked well for thru-hikers, but screw-on fuel canisters are hard to find along the A.T.

Peak 1 *Multi-fuel*: white-gas/kerosene stove, weighs 22oz., requires no setup or priming, self-contained fuel tank and pump, burns 80 minutes on full fuel tank, brings a pint of water to a boil in about 4 minutes, boils 34 pints of water per pint of fuel, good stability, comes with wind screen, offers good simmering characteristics. Other popular models made by Peak 1 include the *Model #442* for burning unleaded gas, the *Feather 400*, and the *Apex Component System*.

Optimus *Svea 123R*: white-gas stove, weighs 20oz., requires no setup but does require priming (optional pump available), self-contained fuel tank, burns 60 minutes at low flame on full fuel tank, brings a pint of water to a boil in about 7 minutes, boils about 25 pints of water per pint of fuel, self-cleaning fuel nozzle, moderate stability, comes with wind screen. Other popular models made by Optimus include the *8R Hunter* and the *1000 Eagle*.

Trangia *Model 27*: alcohol stove, weighs 1lb. 12oz. with nesting cookset (2 pots, 1 frypan, and lid) and wind screen, requires simple setup, burner is non-pressurized open-flame design with no moving parts, burns 25 minutes on full fuel load, brings a pint of water to a boil in about 7 minutes, boils about 28 pints of water per pint of fuel, requires no priming, burns clean, excellent stability, good simmering characteristics. Other popular models made by Trangia include the two-person *Model 25*, and the super-lightweight *Model 28 Mini-Stove* and the *Westwind*.

ZZ Corp. *Sierra Zip*: wood-burning stove, weighs 15oz., requires no setup, unique burning chamber with battery-powered motorized fan (uses AA battery) to feed air to burning fuel, heats like a blacksmith's forge, brings a quart of water to a boil in four minutes, adjustable draft and heat control, burns twigs, bark, pine cones, scrap wood, or charcoal, basic stove available with a variety of cooking kits, offers good stability.

Other: Several generic variations of the above mentioned stove models are seen in catalogues and at yard sales from time to time, but most offer substantially inferior quality and may be dangerous for extended use on a thru-hike. For safety and dependability, you should consider only top-quality stoves and follow the manufacturer's user-instructions to the letter.

Tents

Moss *Starlet*: three-season, 1-2 person, 29 sq. ft. (expands to 37.5 sq. ft. with built-in vestibule on rainfly), 5lbs. 13oz., packed size 5in. x 16in., free-standing overlapping-arc design with two aircraft-aluminum shock-corded poles fitting into generous heavy-duty sleeves, waterproof rip-stop rainfly quickly attachable with snap-in side-release fasteners, fly requires some staking, plenty of headroom over entire area of tent, no-see-um netting to provide good side and top ventilation, interior storage pockets and utility loops for hanging flashlight or clothesline, bathtub floor, and generous stuff sack. Users consider this tent "bombproof" in the severest weather, very durable, can be carried 0.5lb. lighter by substituting lighter stakes. Other popular models made by Moss include the 1-person *Outland/Outland* Netting and 2-person *Stardome II* and *Stargazer*.

Sierra Designs *Clip Flashlight*: three-season, 1-2 person, 32 sq. ft. (expands to 37.5 sq. ft. with built-in vestibule on rainfly), 3lbs. 13oz., packed size 5in. x 17in., modified sphinx-shaped design with two aircraft-aluminum shock-corded poles, tent attaches to poles with quick-clip system, front and rear no-see-um netting for cross-ventilation, interior pockets for storage of small items, good headroom at front end of tent, both tent and fly require staking, and generous stuff sack. Other popular models made by Sierra Designs include the 1-person *Divine Light*, the 2-person *Half Moon Plus*, *Clear Light*, *Sphinx 2*, and *Meteor Light*, and the 2-3-person *Clip 3*.

Eureka! *Timberlite 2*: three-season, 1-2 person, 31 sq. ft. (optional vestibule adds 10 sq. ft.), 4lbs. 11oz., packed size 6in. x 15in., free-standing modified A-frame design with shock-corded aircraft-aluminum poles, tent attaches to poles with quick-clips, hooded rainfly extends down to the ground and requires some staking, no-see-um door and windows to provide cross-ventilation, factory-sealed floor seams, interior mesh storage pockets, gear loft/clothesline rings, and generous stuff sack with pocket for tent poles. Other popular models made by Eureka! include the 1-person *Gossamer*, the 2-person *Backcountry*, *Cirrus*, *Rising Sun*, and *Autumn Wind*, and the 2-3-person *Timberlite 3*.

The North Face *Tadpole NHP*: three-season, 1-2 person, 27 sq. ft. (expands to 32.5 sq. ft. with built-in vestibule on rainfly), 4lbs. 4oz., packed size about 6in. x 18in., free-standing modified sphinx-shaped design using the unique no-hitch-pitch system with tent pre-attached to shock-corded aircraft-aluminum poles for quick setup, waterproof rainfly and floor, rainfly requires some staking, breathable canopy with no-see-um door and windows for ventilation, interior mesh storage pockets, interior hanging loops, and stuff sack. Other popular models made by The North Face include the 2-person *Leafhopper* and *Firefly NHP*, and the 3-person *Bigfrog NHP*.

Bibler *I-Tent*: four-season, 1-2 person, 27.3 sq. ft., 3lbs. 10oz., packed size 6in. x 19in., free-standing single-wall design with two crisscrossing shock-corded aircraft-aluminum poles erected inside the tent for strength, fully factory seam-sealed tent constructed of waterproof breathable fabric, no-see-um door panel for warm weather, bathtub floor with no seams, weatherproof tunnel vent at top of tent for good ventilation, interior odds-and-ends pockets, optional zip-on vestibule, and stuff sack. Other popular models made by Bibler include the 1-person *Solo Dome* and the 2-person *Eldorado*, *Ahwahnee*, *GLT*, and *Phoenix*. A new model, the *Vision 19*, is due out in late 1993 and is worth a look.

Other: Several brands and models that deserve mention, although not quite as frequently seen on the A.T. as those listed above, are REI's *Half Dome*, Kelty's *Windfoil Ultralight*, *Domolite 2*, and *Canyon Ridge*, and Camel's *Journeyman* bivy tent.

Water Filters

Timberline *Timberline*: factory-sealed filter unit with detachable plastic pump, weighs 6oz., filters particles and micro-organisms down to 2 microns nominal, removes the *giardia* cyst but does not protect against bacteria or viruses, filter-capacity is rated at 400 quarts of water per filter, virtually unbreakable, does not affect water taste, pump can be dissembled without tools, can be used as straw.

General Ecology *First-Need*: factory-sealed filter unit with detachable plastic pump, weighs about 12oz., filters particles, bacteria, asbestos fibers, most non-biodegradable chemical pollutants (pesticides, herbicides, *etc.*) down to 0.1 micron nominal, removes the *giardia* cyst but does not remove viruses, filter-capacity not rated but compares favorably with other brands, virtually unbreakable, does not affect water taste, optional prefilter recommended, available in a one-piece *Deluxe* model.

Katadyn *Mini Filter*: one-piece ceramic filter unit and pump, weighs about 8 oz., filters bacteria and micro-organisms down to 0.2 micron nominal, removes the *giardia* cyst but does not remove viruses, filter can be cleaned about 100 times yielding a total output of up to 1000 gallons before a replacement filter unit is needed, does not affect water taste, 30in. suction hose, sturdy construction, recommended for one-person use. The larger *Pocket Filter* is recommended for groups of two or more persons.

MSR *Waterworks*: one-piece 4-stage spongy foam/fine wire mesh, carbon element (or carbon-ceramic)/microporous membrane filter unit and pump, weighs about 18oz., filters bacteria and micro-organisms, herbicides and pesticides down to 0.1 micron nominally, removes the *giardia* cyst but does not remove viruses, cleanable except for replaceable microporous filter, sturdy construction, field maintainable, threaded end of pump screws into wide-mouth water bottle or MSR *Dromedary* water bag.

PUR *Scout*: one-piece fiber/iodine-matrix resin filter unit with pump, weighs about 12oz., optional carbon filter attachment, filters or kills bacteria, micro-organisms including the *giardia cyst*, viruses, and removes many herbicides and pesticides (with carbon filter), disassembles for cleaning and yields about 200 gallons before replacement filter unit is needed, durable construction.

Food Products

Adventure Foods offers a full line of natural bulk-food items and meals prepared especially for backpacking. Owner Jean Spangenberg selects all items herself from around the world. She offers meals especially for use with a BakePacker, and has written a book, *The BakePacker's Companion*, with a wide selection of recipes designed to be blended at home and used by adding only water on the trail. Jean has outfitted many expeditions with food and will work with thru-hikers to plan their food, custom packing and shipping to maildrop locations by arrangement.

Alpineaire offers bulk-food items and a full line of freeze-dried meals for backpacking, with all items free of artificial flavors, colors, and preservatives; available at many retail outfitters.

Wee-Pak offers a full line of freeze-dried lightweight gourmet foods and bulk-food items, all designed to be used by adding only water and cooking. Assistance in planning menus, and custom shipping to specified pickup points is available by arrangement.

Richmoor offers a full line of bulk-food items and freeze-dried and dehydrated meals, with their *Natural High* brand featuring natural foods free of artificial flavors, colors, and preservatives; available at many retail outfitters.

Women's Clothing

Zanika Sportswear offers a line of outdoor wear designed specially for active women by an active sports-woman (Vickie Morgan), and field tested by women doing various outdoor activities. Many items feature a unique "women's fly" that allows the user to answer the call of nature without having to undress.

Address of Manufacturers/Distributors

The names and addresses of the manufacturers and/or distributors of popular products used on the A.T. are listed below. Following the name, the product(s) they make are listed in italics, sometimes with the following abbreviations to conserve space: Bp=backpacks, Cl=clothing and rainwear, Sb=sleeping bags, Sp=sleeping pads, Stv=stoves, Tnt=tents, Wf=water filters, Wb=water bottles.

Adventure Foods *(food)*
Rt. 2, Box 276
Whittier, NC 28789
704-497-4113

Alpineaire *(food)*
P. O. Box 1600
Nevada City, CA 95959
1-800-322-6325

BakePacker *(bread baker)*
Rt. 2, Box 276
Whittier, NC 28789
704-497-4113

Bibler Tents *(Tnt)*
5441-D Western Avenue
Boulder, CO 80301
303-449-7351

Birkenstock *(sandals)*
P. O. Box 6140
Novato, CA 94948
1-800-597-3338

Brunton *(compasses)*
620 E. Monroe Avenue
Riverton, WY 82501
307-856-6559

Camp Trails *(Bp)*
P. O. Box 966
Binghamton, NY 13902
607-779-2200

Caribou Mt'neering *(Sb)*
P. O. Box 3696
Chico, CA 95927
1-800-824-4153

Carinthia/Gold-Eck *(Sb)*
6313 Seaview Avenue N.W.
Seattle, WA 98107
206-781-0886

Dana Design, Ltd. *(Bp)*
1950 North 19th Avenue
Bozeman, MT 59715
406-587-4188

Danner Boots *(boots)*
12722 N.E. Airport Way
Portland, OR 97230
1-800-345-0430

Earth Pad/Gemini *(Sp)*
P. O. Box 398
Beverly, MA 01915
1-800-828-2868

Eureka! Tent *(Tnt)*
P. O. Box 966
Binghamton, NY 13902
607-779-2200

First-Need *(Wf)*
151 Sheree Boulevard
Exton, PA 19341
215-363-7900

Fox River *(hiking socks)*
P. O. Box 298
Osage, IA 50461
515-732-3798

Gregory Mtn. Products *(Bp)*
100 Calle Cortez
Temecula, CA 92390
714-676-5621

Hi-Tec Sports USA *(boots)*
4801 Stoddard Road
Modesto, CA 93536
1-800-521-1698

JanSport, Inc. *(Bp/Cl)*
10411 Airport Road S.W.
Everett, WA 98204
1-800-426-9227

Katadyn USA, Inc. *(Wf)*
3020 North Scottsdale Road
Scottsdale, AZ 85251
602-990-3131

Kelty Pack, Inc. *(Bp/Tnt/Sb)*
P. O. Box 7048-A
St. Louis, MO 63177
1-800-423-2320

Limmer & Sons *(boots)*
P. O. Box 88
Intervale, NH 03845
603-356-5378

Leki *(hiking sticks)*
60 Earhart Drive - Unit 18
Williamsville, NY 14221
1-800-255-9982

Lowe Alpine Products *(Bp)*
P. O. Box 1449
Broomfield, CO 80038
303-465-3706

Marmot Mountain *(Sb/Cl)*
2321 Circadian Way
Santa Rosa, CA 95407
707-544-4590

McHale & Company *(Bp)*
29 Dravus Street
Seattle, WA 98109
206-281-7861

Merrell USA *(boots)*
P. O. Box 4249
South Burlington, VT 05406
1-800-869-3348

Moonstone *(Sb/Cl)*
5350 Ericson Way
Arcata, CA 95521
707-822-2985

Moss, Inc. (Tnt)
P. O. Box 309
Camden, ME 04843
1-800-341-1557

Mountainsmith, Inc. (Bp)
Heritage Square, Building P
Golden, CO 80401
303-279-5930

MSR (Stv/Wf)
P. O. Box 24547
Seattle, WA 98124
206-682-4184

Nalgene Trail Products (Wb)
Box 20365
Rochester, NY 14602
716-586-8800

One Sport (boots)
1003 Sixth Avenue South
Seattle, WA 98134
206-621-9303

Optimus/Suunto USA (Stv)
2151 Las Palmas Drive
Carlsbad, CA 92009
619-931-6788

Patagonia (Cl)
Box 150
Ventura, CA 93002
805-643-8616

Peak 1/Coleman (Stv/Sb/Bp)
P. O. Box 2931
Wichita, KS 67201
316-261-3211

Petzl/Pigeon Mtn. (headlamp)
P. O. Box 803
LaFayette, GA 30728
706-764-1437

Powerfood (Power Bars)
1442A Walnut Street
Berkeley, CA 94709
1-800-444-5154

PUR (Wf)
2229 Edgewood Avenue South
Minneapolis, MN 55426
1-800-845-7873

Raichle USA, Inc. (boots)
Geneva Road
Brewster, NY 10509
914-279-5121

Richmoor/Natural High (food)
P. O. Box 8092
Van Nuys, CA 91409
1-800-423-3170

Sierra Designs (Tnt/Sb/Cl)
2039 Fourth Street
Berkeley, CA 94710
1-800-423-6363

Silva Compass (compasses)
P. O. Box 966
Binghamton, NY 13902
607-779-2200

Slumberjack (Sb)
P. O. Box 7048-A
St. Louis, MO 63177
1-800-233-6283

Spenco (footcare products)
P. O. Box 2501
Waco, TX 76702
1-800-877-3626

Sqwincher (electrolyte drink)
P. O. Box 192
Columbus, MS 39703
1-800-654-1920

Swiss Army Brands (knives)
Box 874
Shelton, CT 06484
1-800-243-4032

Tecnica (boots)
19 Technology Drive
West Lebanon, NH 03784
1-800-258-3897

Teva (sandals)
P. O. Box 5022
Carpinteria, CA 93014
805-684-6694

The North Face (Bp/Tnt/Sb/Cl)
999 Harrison Street
Berkeley, CA 94710
510-527-9700

Therm·A·Rest (Sp)
4000 1st Avenue S.
Seattle, WA 98134
206-583-0583

Thor·Lo Socks (hiking socks)
P. O. Box 5440
Statesville, NC 28677
1-800-438-0209

Timberline Filters, Inc. (Wf)
P. O. Box 12007
Boulder, CO 80303
303-494-4104

Tracks (hiking sticks)
4000 1st Avenue S.
Seattle, WA 98134
206-583-0583

Trangia/Denali Intl. (Stv)
Box 599
Waterbury, VT 05676
1-800-522-2519

Vasque Shoe Co. (boots)
314 Main Street
Red Wing, MN 55066
1-800-359-2668

WeePak (food)
P. O. Box 562
Sun Valley, ID 83353
1-800-722-2710

Wiggy's Inc. (Sb)
P. O. Box 2124
Grand Junction, CO 81502
303-241-6465

Wigwam (hiking socks)
3402 Crocker Avenue
Sheboygan, WI 53081
414-457-5551

Zanika Sportswear (clothing)
4315 Oliver Avenue North
Minneapolis, MN 55412
(612) 521-1429

ZZ Corp. (Zzip stove)
10806 Kaylor Street
Los Alamitos, CA 90720
510-598-3220

Workbook Section

This section contains a blank set of planning forms, identical to the ones illustrated in the "Sample Planning Notebook" section of this guide. These forms will allow you to record your planning details in a systematic manner, so that information can be easily retrieved when you begin assembling the physical components needed for doing your hike.

More than enough space is provided for planning a "normal" thru-hike, so, if you find the details of your hike (e.g., number of maildrops) are too numerous to fit on these forms, you may want to reexamine your plans and simplify them. Feel free to make additional copies of these planning forms for your private use as you do your planning. However, I do request that you not distribute duplicate copies of these blank planning forms to anyone else.

If you have questions or problems during your planning, or if you just get excited about your trip and want to talk to someone about it, remember that you can call me at (704) 622-7601. Please try to limit calls to the hours between 7:30 p.m. and 9:30 p.m., Eastern Time.

GOOD LUCK WITH YOUR PLANNING!

Equipment Checklist

WEIGHT (in ounces)		ITEMS CARRIED IN BACKPACK (at beginning of hike)	DESCRIPTION OF ITEMS (make, model, size, etc.)
		Backpack (empty) w/belt, accessories	
		Raincover for backpack	
		Tent (or tarp) w/accessories	
		Plastic groundsheet to fit under tent (opt.)	
		Sleeping bag w/stuff sack and garbage bag	
		Sleeping pad w/nylon carrying sack	
		Groundcloth, nylon (opt.)	
		Sitting pad (opt.)	
		Stove (empty)	
		Fuel bottle (empty)	
		Cookset (pots, pans, potholder, etc.)	
		Cooking utensils (excluding knife)	
		Butane lighter (or matches)	
		Water bottle(s), 1-pint (wide-mouth)	
		Water bottle(s), 1-quart (wide-mouth)	
		Water bag, 1-2 gallon carrying capacity	
		Water purifier (chemical or filter type)	
		First-aid kit (from Kits Checklist)	
		Grooming kit (from Kits Checklist)	
		Toilet kit (from Kits Checklist)	
		Misc./repair kit (from Kits Checklist)	
		Sewing kit (from Kits Checklist)	
		Knife	
		Flashlight w/batteries	
		Candle lantern and/or candle (opt.)	
		Compass	
		Whistle	
		Cord (1/8" diameter x 50' in length)	
		Camera w/batteries (opt.)	
		Camera kit (from Kits Checklist)	
		Radio or cassette player (opt.)	
		Datapouch (guidebooks, journal, pen, etc.)	
		Clothing (from Clothing Checklist)	
		Fuel (1 fluid oz. = 0.8 oz. weight)	
		Water (1 pint = 16 oz. weight)	
None		Hiking stick (hand carried, no pack weight)	
		TOTAL ESTIMATED PACK WEIGHT (without food) = (_____ lbs. _____ ozs.)	

W-1

Kits Checklist

First-aid Kit
Weight: _____ ounces

- [ ] Aspirin (or equivalent)
- [ ] Antibiotic ointment
- [ ] Skin cream or Vaseline, small tube (opt.)
- [ ] Cortisone cream (opt.)
- [ ] Eyedrops (Visine or equivalent)
- [ ] Toothache medicine (opt.)
- [ ] Athlete's foot medicine
- [ ] Powder (for chafing)
- [ ] Antacid tablets
- [ ] Lip balm (Chapstick or Blistex)
- [ ] Diarrhea medicine (opt.)
- [ ] Allergy medicine (opt.)
- [ ] Bandaids (a few for minor cuts)
- [ ] Gauze, 1"-wide roll
- [ ] Sterile pads, 2"x2" (a few for larger cuts)
- [ ] Sterile pad, large (a few for bigger wounds)
- [ ] Adhesive tape (or surgical tape)
- [ ] Ace bandage (2"-wide)
- [ ] Moleskin or equivalent
- [ ] Second Skin by Spenco (opt.)
- [ ] Scissors, manicure type (opt.)
- [ ] Tweezers (opt.)
- [ ] Snakebite kit (opt.)

Grooming Kit
Weight: _____ ounces

- [ ] Toothbrush
- [ ] Toothpaste
- [ ] Dental floss
- [ ] Biodegradeable soap
- [ ] Deodorant (opt.)
- [ ] Comb (opt.)
- [ ] Hair brush (opt.)
- [ ] Nail clippers
- [ ] Razor (opt.)
- [ ] Mirror (opt.)
- [ ] Washcloth (opt.)
- [ ] Towel (opt.)

Toilet Kit
Weight: _____ ounces

- [ ] Toilet paper (in Ziploc bag)
- [ ] Tampons/sanitary napkins
- [ ] Matches
- [ ] Trowel (opt.)

Miscellaneous/repair Kit
Weight: _____ ounces

- [ ] Spare parts for backpack
- [ ] Therm-A-Rest repair kit
- [ ] Extra flashlight bulb(s)
- [ ] Stove repair kit
- [ ] Extra batteries   (AAA)   (AA)   (C)   (9v)
- [ ] Boot glue
- [ ] Boot waterproofing

Sewing Kit
Weight: _____ ounces

- [ ] Needles
- [ ] Top-stitching thread (black)
- [ ] Regular thread (wrapped around paper)
- [ ] Thimble, plastic
- [ ] Buttons (a few to match clothing)
- [ ] Safety pins (a few, assorted sizes)

Camera Kit
Weight: _____ ounces

- [ ] Lens paper
- [ ] Lens cleaning solution (opt.)
- [ ] Lens blower-brush
- [ ] Tabletop tripod (opt.)
- [ ] Film, ASA#   (100)   (200)   (400)
- [ ] Film, ASA#   (100)   (200)   (400)
- [ ] Film, ASA#   (100)   (200)   (400)

Clothing and Footwear Checklist

WEIGHT (in ounces)	CLOTHING ITEMS CARRIED IN BACKPACK (at beginning of hike)	Qty.	DESCRIPTION OF ITEMS (brand, size, color, etc.)
	Hiking footwear:		
	Hiking socks		
	Sock liners		
	Warm-weather clothing:		
	Hiking shorts		
	Underpants/bra (opt.)		
	Hiking shirts, short-sleeve		
	Hiking shirts, long-sleeve		
	Pants, long (opt.)		
	Sweater, lightweight (or equivalent garment)		
	Jacket, lightweight (or equivalent garment)		
	Cold-weather clothing:		
	Underpants, thermal		
	Undershirts, thermal		
	Sweater, heavy (or equivalent garment)		
	Parka, lined (or equivalent garment)		
	Ski cap, wool (or equivalent garment)		
	Gloves		
	Rainwear:		
	Rainpants		
	Rain jacket		
	Poncho		
	Gaiters		
	Town clothes:		
	Sneakers or sandals		
	Town socks (opt.)		
	Town shirt (opt.)		
	Town pants (opt.)		
	Accessories:		
	Wallet		
	Clothes bag w/plastic bag liner		
	TOTAL ESTIMATED CLOTHING WEIGHT (in pack) = (_____ lbs. _____ ozs.)		

Clothing and Footwear Checklist

(page 2)

ITEMS WORN TO START HIKE (assuming warm weather)	Qty.	DESCRIPTION OF ITEMS: (brand, size, color, etc.)
Hiking boots		
Hiking socks		
Sock liners (opt.)		
Hiking shirt, short sleeve		
Hiking shorts		
Hat or cap (opt.)		
Bandana		
Wristwatch (opt.)		

Note: Do not include the weight of the above items in the clothing weight recorded on your Equipment Checklist, since these items will not be carried in your pack. However, do not forget to include them when calculating quantities of clothing to purchase for your trip.

Clothing and footwear items to be packed in maildrops:

MD#	Maildrop Location	Clothing and Footwear Items

Note: Northbounders should pick up extra cold-weather items for going through the White Mountains at Hanover or Glencliff, New Hampshire. Southbounders usually pick up cold-weather items no later than Damascus, Virginia, and, depending on the year, may need them earlier.

Menu Planner

Meal #	Breakfast	Lunch	Supper	Snacks
1				
2				
3				
4				
5				

Food List

Meal	Food Item	Servings Needed	Amount per Serving	Total Amount	Unit Price	Total Cost
BREAKFAST						
LUNCH						
SUPPER						
SNACKS						
					Total Estimated Cost	

Supplies and Misc. Items Lists

Supplies	Used on the Trail for:	Number Needed	Unit Price	Total Cost
		Total Estimated Cost		

Misc. Items	Used on the Trail for:	Number Needed	Unit Price	Total Cost
		Total Estimated Cost		

Hiking Schedule
(page 1)

Day #	Date	Day	Miles	Destination	MD#	B	L	S

Key to symbols and abbreviations: **MD**=maildrop, **B**=breakfast, **L**=lunch, **S**=supper, **X**=meal from maildrop, **G**=meal from grocery store, **R**=meal from restaurant, **A**=meal included in price of lodging (American plan)

Hiking Schedule
(page 2)

Day #	Date	Day	Miles	Destination	MD#	B	L	S

Key to symbols and abbreviations: **MD**=maildrop, **B**=breakfast, **L**=lunch, **S**=supper, **X**=meal from maildrop, **G**=meal from grocery store, **R**=meal from restaurant, **A**=meal included in price of lodging (American plan)

Hiking Schedule
(page 3)

Day #	Date	Day	Miles	Destination	MD#	B	L	S

Key to symbols and abbreviations: **MD**=maildrop, **B**=breakfast, **L**=lunch, **S**=supper, **X**=meal from maildrop, **G**=meal from grocery store, **R**=meal from restaurant, **A**=meal included in price of lodging (American plan)

Hiking Schedule
(page 4)

Day #	Date	Day	Miles	Destination	MD#	B	L	S

Key to symbols and abbreviations: **MD**=maildrop, **B**=breakfast, **L**=lunch, **S**=supper, **X**=meal from maildrop, **G**=meal from grocery store, **R**=meal from restaurant, **A**=meal included in price of lodging (American plan)

Hiking Schedule
(page 5)

Day #	Date	Day	Miles	Destination	MD#	B	L	S

Key to symbols and abbreviations: **MD**=maildrop, **B**=breakfast, **L**=lunch, **S**=supper, **X**=meal from maildrop, **G**=meal from grocery store, **R**=meal from restaurant, **A**=meal included in price of lodging (American plan)

Hiking Schedule
(page 6)

Day #	Date	Day	Miles	Destination	MD#	B	L	S

Key to symbols and abbreviations: **MD**=maildrop, **B**=breakfast, **L**=lunch, **S**=supper, **X**=meal from maildrop, **G**=meal from grocery store, **R**=meal from restaurant, **A**=meal included in price of lodging (American plan)

Maildrop Packing List

		Number of breakfasts needed in each maildrop	Breakfast items to be packed in maildrop:
MD#	**Maildrop Location**		
	Totals		

W-14

Maildrop Packing List

		Lunch	Number of lunches needed in each maildrop	Lunch items to be packed in maildrop:											
MD#	Maildrop Location														
	Totals														

Maildrop Packing List

	Supper	Number of suppers needed in each maildrop	Supper items to be packed in maildrop:											
MD#	Maildrop Location													
	Totals													

Maildrop Packing List

Other Foods

Other foods to be packed in maildrop:

MD#	Maildrop Location														
	Totals														

Maildrop Packing List

		Supplies to be packed in maildrop:
Supplies		
MD#	Maildrop Location	
	Totals	

Maildrop Packing List

Misc. Items		Misc. items to be packed in maildrop:												
MD#	Maildrop Location													
	Totals													

Maildrop Posting Schedule

MD#	Maildrop Location	ZIP Code	Due Date	Mailing Date

Mailing Instructions:

All packages sent to post offices should be addressed as follows:

Your Name
c/o General Delivery
City, State, ZIP Code

Place the phrase "Hold for A.T. Hiker" (and your expected due date) in lower left corner of package or label.

WARNING!—Do not send maildrop packages to post offices via UPS or Federal Express, since postal personnel are prevented by law from accepting or holding such private-carrier packages.

List of Accommodations

Pack in MD#	Location (town and lodging facility)	# of nights	$ per night	Total $
				Total Estimated Cost

Budget Planner

		Grocery Stores			Restaurants								
Budgeting for Meals Lodging etc.		Breakfasts @ $____ per meal	Lunches @ $____ per meal	Suppers @ $____ per meal	Breakfasts @ $____ per meal	Lunches @ $____ per meal	Suppers @ $____ per meal	Lodging costs (from List of Accommodations)	Miscellaneous expenses (estimate)	Fun money (estimate)			TOTALS
MD#	Maildrop Location												

Total Estimated Cost

W-22

Back-up Gear List

Equipment:

1. _____
2. _____
3. _____
4. _____
5. _____
6. _____
7. _____
8. _____
9. _____
10. _____
11. _____
12. _____
13. _____
14. _____
15. _____
16. _____
17. _____
18. _____
19. _____
20. _____
21. _____
22. _____
23. _____
24. _____
25. _____
26. _____
27. _____
28. _____
29. _____
30. _____
31. _____
32. _____
33. _____
34. _____
35. _____
36. _____

Clothing/Footwear:

37. _____
38. _____
39. _____
40. _____
41. _____
42. _____
43. _____
44. _____
45. _____
46. _____
47. _____
48. _____
49. _____
50. _____
51. _____
52. _____
53. _____
54. _____
55. _____
56. _____
57. _____
58. _____
59. _____
60. _____
61. _____
62. _____
63. _____
64. _____
65. _____
66. _____
67. _____
68. _____
69. _____
70. _____
71. _____
72. _____